"Social networks are evolving into commercial networks—a way to find jobs and conduct work—and thus are an increasingly important channel in people's lives. As Wayne points out in his excellent book, LinkedIn is all about making the right connections, which is why we view it as an invaluable tool for recruiting talent that helps our clients win. Buy at least 396 copies of Wayne's book and share it with all your friends."

—Mark Toth, chief legal officer, Manpower North America

"I know of no one who knows how to use LinkedIn better than Wayne Breitbarth. That he is willing to share his knowledge so clearly and concisely is truly a gift—his gift to anyone who needs to connect for business, for fun, or to find a job."

—Robert Grede, bestselling author of *Naked Marketing* and *The Spur & The Sash*

"I own a small business and have followed Wayne's advice to better utilize LinkedIn. By revising my profile, participating in groups, and more effectively using the advanced search function, I've been able to get connected to key decision-makers and drive traffic to our website. It's been a great business development tool for my company."

—Jeff Carrigan, founder and CMO, Big Shoes Network

"*The Power Formula* greatly simplifies the ability of those of us not in the Facebook generation to make sense of social media and leverage LinkedIn for business success."

—Michael A. Dalton, author of *Simplifying Innovation*

"This book is just like Wayne himself—smart, down-to-earth, and full of good ideas. *The Power Formula for LinkedIn Success* explains how anyone can use LinkedIn to propel business growth. With clear explanations and real-life examples, it's a must-read for anyone who is serious about business development."

—Christina Steder, president, Clear Verve Marketing

"While college students are not strangers to social media, having direction and focus on how to appropriately and professionally use LinkedIn as a tool for researching careers and networking with professionals is essential. Wayne Breitbarth gives great instruction for this tech-savvy yet new-to-the-workforce population."

—Laura F. Kestner, director, Career Services Center, Marquette University

"The combination of Wayne Breitbarth's passion for the power of social networking and his real-world business experience, deep knowledge, mastery of LinkedIn, and skill as a trainer make the *The Power Formula for LinkedIn Success* a real standout. This is the one book to buy if you are serious about getting up to speed fast."

—Frank Martinelli, president, The Center for P

NAN

D0424182

"As someone who has been helping clients use the Web and social media as powerful business tools for fifteen years, I'm embarrassed to admit that I never quite 'got' LinkedIn. It wasn't until some of my public speaking engagements had me on the same program with Wayne that I realized what I was missing. Wayne's real-world experience, commonsense approach, and enthusiastic style have turned roomfuls of attendees—and me—into true believers in the power of LinkedIn. I still help my clients with their Facebook, Twitter, and Foursquare tactics, but for LinkedIn expertise that translates into meaningful results, I send them to see Wayne. If LinkedIn is just a part of your business social media strategy, Wayne's book will be valuable. And if LinkedIn is the only thing you do, it's the only book you need!"

—Tom Snyder, president and CEO, Trivera Interactive, and author of *The Complete Idiot's Mini Guide to Real-time Marketing with Foursquare*

"Wayne's delightful book will help you build competence in understanding LinkedIn, gain confidence in using this important tool, and enable you to take the risk of embracing social media to advance your professional goals. Buy it today!"

—Susan Marshall, president, Executive Advisor LLC, and author of *How to Grow a Backbone*

"A worthwhile business book is one that gets turned into a reference guide to be referred to over and over. Wayne has written such a book. Buy one and you'll be less intimidated about Web 2.0, Sales 2.0, and you'll begin to get measurable results from one social media option—because you'll be linked in!"

—Jeff Koser, author of *Selling to Zebras*

"Wayne Breitbarth unlocks the secrets to successfully using one of the most important business tools in today's arsenal: LinkedIn. *The Power Formula for LinkedIn Success* is a practical tool for anyone looking to significantly improve their career, business, or professional standing. Breitbarth's Power Formula provides a simple and easy-to-use method for increasing visibility through one of today's most popular digital platforms. His down-to-earth writing style combined with loads of LinkedIn insights makes this a must-have book for anyone not wanting to get passed by on today's digital business superhighway."

—Rich Horwath, author of *Deep Dive: The Proven Method for Building Strategy, Focusing Your Resources, and Taking Smart Action*

"If you've asked 'Where's the value of LinkedIn?' or 'Why should I invest the time to use LinkedIn?' then you need to read Wayne's book! His Power Formula provides brilliant insight and guidance on how to get started using the LinkedIn platform to get your arms around the most powerful asset you have—your network of relationships. Whether you are averse to technology, or an executive with little time to spare, Wayne will show you where the value is!"

—Michael Kuhlman, president, 123Smarket.com

The Power Formula for

LinkedIn

Success

NANUET PUBLIC LIBRARY
149 Church Street
Nanuet, NY 10954
845-623-4281

The Power Formula for

LinkedIn

Success

Kick-start Your Business, Brand, *and* Job Search

Wayne Breitbarth

GREENLEAF
BOOK GROUP PRESS

NANUET PUBLIC LIBRARY
149 Church Street
Nanuet, NY 10954
845-623-4281

This publication is designed to provide accurate and authoritative information in regard to the subject matter covered. It is sold with the understanding that the publisher and author are not engaged in rendering legal, accounting, or other professional services. If legal advice or other expert assistance is required, the services of a competent professional should be sought.

Every effort has been made to make this book as complete and as accurate as possible, but no warranty of fitness is implied. The information provided is on an "as is" basis. The author and publisher shall have neither liability nor responsibility to any person or entity with respect to any loss or damages arising from the information contained in the book. The reader should be aware that the LinkedIn website as listed and shown in this work may have changed or disappeared between when this work was written and when it is read, and the author and publisher shall not be held liable for consequences relating to the elimination of information or changes to this website.

LinkedIn is a registered trademark of LinkedIn Corporation. The author is not associated with any product or vendor mentioned in this book unless otherwise noted. LinkedIn does not endorse any of the material contained herein.

Published by Greenleaf Book Group Press
Austin, Texas
www.gbgpress.com

Copyright ©2011 Wayne Breitbarth

All rights reserved.

No part of this book may be reproduced, stored in a retrieval system, or transmitted by any means, electronic, mechanical, photocopying, recording, or otherwise, without written permission from the publisher.

Distributed by Greenleaf Book Group LLC

For ordering information or special discounts for bulk purchases, please contact Greenleaf Book Group LLC at PO Box 91869, Austin, TX 78709, 512.891.6100.

Design and composition by Greenleaf Book Group LLC and Publications Development Company
Cover design by Greenleaf Book Group LLC

Publisher's Cataloging-In-Publication Data
(Prepared by The Donohue Group, Inc.)
Breitbarth, Wayne.
    The power formula for LinkedIn success : kick-start your business, brand, and job search / Wayne Breitbarth -- 1st ed.
    p. ; cm.
    ISBN: 978-1-60832-093-6
    1. LinkedIn (Electronic resource) 2. Online social networks. 3. Business networks--Computer network resources. 4. Branding (Marketing)--Computer network resources. 5. Job hunting--Computer network resources. 6. Success in business. I. Title.
HD30.37 B74 2011
658.054678   2010914413

Part of the Tree Neutral™ program, which offsets the number of trees consumed in the production and printing of this book by taking proactive steps, such as planting trees in direct proportion to the number of trees used: www.treeneutral.com

Printed in the United States of America on acid-free paper

10 11 12 13 14 15   10 9 8 7 6 5 4 3 2 1

First Edition

Contents

About This Book

This book is meant to help you quickly, efficiently, and painlessly discover whether this thing called LinkedIn is worth your time and effort and to understand how to effectively use it to accomplish your business goals. You may choose to read it cover to cover or immediately begin applying the techniques and strategies discussed in each chapter. In either case, it will be an important reference as you move from novice to experienced user. I sincerely hope you will find this book to be motivational, educational, and entertaining.

As with most Internet-based resources, there will be periodic updates and other changes to the LinkedIn website. In order for this book to remain relevant and accurate, I will address these modifications on my website: www.powerformula.net. Visit the website as well for tips, suggestions, and other helpful resources to assist you in using LinkedIn to successfully brand and market yourself and your business.

Introduction

I Never Even Wanted to Be on LinkedIn!

I never wanted to be on LinkedIn, never thought it would be useful, and surely never wanted to spend a significant amount of time teaching other business executives how to use it. I am not someone who loves technology for technology's sake; I am an experienced businessperson who respects the experience and knowledge of other businesspeople. Business professionals tend to be interested in thoroughly exploring the "why" before launching into the "how to." Thus, this book is designed to not only teach you how to effectively use LinkedIn but also to show you why the tools, techniques, and strategies presented here can be instrumental in furthering your professional goals. With that in mind, let me share with you some background on my LinkedIn journey and explain why I think LinkedIn is an important tool for you to investigate and master.

Think back to the time you received your very first e-mail. If you were like me, you looked at that e-mail and said, "Nah, this will never work. People will never communicate this way, and

I'm sure if I ignore this, it will just go away." Well, do you know anyone today who doesn't have an e-mail account? Can you even imagine going a day (or perhaps even a couple of hours) without checking your e-mail?

In my opinion, the whole social media phenomenon, and LinkedIn in particular, has that same kind of feel to it. Although I am not a futurist, it's clear that the process of connecting with people over the Internet is here to stay. When people attend my training classes, especially people in my age group (as of this writing, I am fifty-three years old), many of them hope the ninety minutes they spend will confirm their suspicion that this tool is worthless or avoidable. It may be your secret desire (or maybe your not-so-secret desire) that when you finish this book, you'll be able to confidently say, "Great. No value there. Now I can move on. My life is too busy for LinkedIn anyway!"

That is why I approach my training classes as well as this book with the intention of not necessarily teaching you every specific technique of using LinkedIn but instead showing you its capabilities so that you can get rid of the fear factor. I suspect that fear comes from two sources: Potential users ask themselves, "What will happen if I jump into the murky waters of LinkedIn?" or, more importantly, "Will I be at a competitive disadvantage if my competitors embrace this technology while I sit on the fence?" My goal is for you to end up in one of three camps after reading this book. First, you may gain an understanding of the concept and recognize what you might be missing but choose instead to spend your time finding another way to brand or market yourself and your business. That's fine. LinkedIn isn't necessarily for everyone. Second, once you have a better understanding of the capabilities of LinkedIn, you may decide to either tinker with it on a limited basis or strategize about how you may be able to use it to advance your career or business in a few key ways. Or, third, you may decide this is a rockin' tool, even for a person your age, and realize that you'd better get on board completely—and also have people in your company fully understand its concepts, premises, and working parts.

LinkedIn is all about using the Internet to find and be found by people—in addition to using the good old-fashioned face-to-face method of meeting people. Perhaps over time more personal contact will be replaced with virtual interactions, but LinkedIn will never completely take the place of meeting people in your business sphere and spending time with them, either on the phone or in person. People still prefer to do business with people they know and trust, and typically knowing and trusting takes place much more rapidly when contact occurs on a face-to-face basis.

None of us is looking for another thing to do for two or three hours each week to replace spending time with our families, playing golf, fishing, or engaging in other hobbies we enjoy. Therefore, my hope is that the time you spend on LinkedIn will not necessarily add a burden to your already busy lives but that it will allow you to do a form of networking 24/7, perhaps while watching your favorite TV shows or sporting events. Being a Wisconsinite, it is my duty to watch the Green Bay Packers play football on TV each Sunday afternoon. However, I have within me this nagging little voice that says, *Wayne, this is not a very productive endeavor*, especially when the Packers are getting annihilated. Now, with the help of my laptop, LinkedIn allows me to keep track of what is going on in my network of professionals, while at the same time keeping an eye on the Packers game.

LinkedIn is the world's largest online business networking site. You join LinkedIn either by going to LinkedIn.com and setting up an account or by accepting an invitation from someone who has suggested you sign up. Most people are invited by several friends or business associates before making the decision to join LinkedIn, and it usually takes an invitation from a very trusted friend before they get started. However, even after they take the first step, it's common for people to not really know what or why they are joining; they simply check the box and begin the journey without either knowing what LinkedIn does or having a strategy for how to use it.

By the time this book hits the shelves, LinkedIn will have around 100 million users, with one new member being added every second of the day. Fifty percent of those members are in the United States. The following chart enumerates some interesting statistics relating to the demographics of LinkedIn users:

THE LINKEDIN PROFESSIONAL AT A GLANCE

Average Age	43
Male/Female	54% / 46%
College Grad/Post Grad	77.6%
Business Decision Maker	49%
Average Household Income	$107,278
Household Income $100K+	51.8%

Source: Nielsen Online @ Plan, Summer 2009,
taken from http://advertising.linkedin.com/audience

Here's how I got started on LinkedIn. I have a very close friend who nagged me Sunday after Sunday at church, explaining that I should get on LinkedIn, and I consistently blew him off, saying, "I don't have time to keep track of your LinkedIn or Plaxo or Facebook or any other website." Yet he consistently said to me, "Listen—you are a small business owner and you really need this."

Well, as luck would have it, one afternoon I found myself stuck in a hotel room in a remote location with nothing to do. It's not my style to spend the afternoon watching TV, so I thought I would check out this LinkedIn thing and see what it was about. Two hours later, I had overcome my fear and ordered two books about LinkedIn from Amazon.com. I now saw LinkedIn as a powerful tool and wanted to become an expert as soon as humanly possible. Four or five hours later, in that same hotel room, I was en route to becoming a passionate proponent of virtual networking. I immediately began connecting with people from my past, including college classmates and employees of many of the companies I had worked with in the Milwaukee area over the past thirty years.

In response to my newfound enthusiasm, friends and colleagues began asking me questions about LinkedIn. After admitting I had become a LinkedIn junkie, I would invite them into our company's boardroom and spend time sharing what I knew about LinkedIn with them. This turned into a formal class, which I now offer several times per month, and has also led to speaking engagements with groups such as chambers of commerce, professional associations, and Rotary Clubs, as well as small and medium-sized businesses.

Despite the fact that LinkedIn is often referred to as "Facebook for businesspeople," what businesspeople appreciate and respect about LinkedIn is that it has significant processes and controls that keep it from becoming like Facebook. At the time of this writing, Facebook has over half a billion members, and the ability to connect with such a vast number of people certainly does attract some businesspeople. However, many facets of Facebook—such as pictures of your past tagged with your name (and possibly including beer bongs and bikinis), relationship statuses, and religious and political views—are things that totally turn off most businesspeople to using the site for professional networking. Facebook does have applications for certain types of businesses (those that sell directly to consumers), but many businesspeople feel more comfortable with LinkedIn because of its built-in controls and personal settings. I will discuss many of those controls and settings in subsequent chapters of this book.

By now you are, no doubt, anxious to get started. So fasten your seatbelt and prepare to see your fear subside as you learn more about what LinkedIn is and how it can help you kick-start your business, brand, and job search.

CHAPTER 1

A New Way to Look at Social Media

The LinkedIn Power Formula

I had been on LinkedIn for just over a year and had taught more than 120 classes, with over four thousand participants, when I had a revelation: All of these social media tools are just that—tools! No different than a hammer, which is only as good as the person swinging it. As I started to think about this more and more, I realized that there is one group of people—we will call them the Facebook generation—and then there are the rest of us, the non-Facebook generation. The first group is darned good at social media and grasp it so much more easily than we do, since they grew up with the Internet. They embrace new social technologies in a big hurry, which scares the heck out of those of us in the non-Facebook group. So, instead of deciding we should get on board, we just hope it will go away, thinking that maybe we'll wake up one day, it will all be gone, and things will be back to "normal."

I'm not telling you this because I want to bring you down even further but because I have some good news about the person swinging the hammer: you. You already have lots of experience and relationships that you can leverage to make your use of LinkedIn—or any other social media site—much more effective. It is this revelation that helped me come up with the idea of the Power Formula:

Your Unique Experience + Your Unique Relationships + The Tool (in this case, LinkedIn) = The Power

Anyone with business experience and the willingness to learn can realize great benefits from LinkedIn. And getting started with LinkedIn is really not that big of a deal: You can either read a book about how to use LinkedIn, attend a seminar, consult an expert you trust, or check out the Learning Center on LinkedIn.com. Learn as much as you can, and then take the time to execute the strategies you have been shown. Make the commitment to get this done, and make it a priority to establish some good Linked-In habits. No matter how tech-savvy they are, members of the Facebook generation cannot go to a two-hour seminar and come away with the wealth of experience and relationships that comes from years of meetings, handshakes, small talk, weekend retreats, planning sessions, bad proposals, good proposals, winning jobs, losing jobs, etc. But members of the non-Facebook generations, who have the benefit of these experiences and relationships, can be right where they want to be after just one weekend and an ongoing commitment to a LinkedIn strategy. That's how I started two short years ago. I got on LinkedIn.com, bought a few books, digested the information, and was on my way to creating my own LinkedIn strategy.

Let me address the components of the Power Formula in greater detail so you can better grasp its importance.

Your Unique Experience

Every one of us has unique experiences that we bring to the marketplace. These experiences include our education, jobs, culture, ethnicity, interests, and family, to name a few. Today, with virtual marketing and promotion more important than ever, developing a strong personal brand is essential, and your unique experience is a substantial component of that brand. The longer you have been in the marketplace, the more experiences you have amassed, each of which may come to bear on your next business opportunity.

Your Unique Relationships

Because none of us has walked the same path or encountered the same people, we have each developed a unique set of relationships. These relationships have been the foundation of our friendships, business partnerships, and customer bases. When we need help, whether personally or professionally, we turn to these people—our network. They in turn know that we are just a phone call away when we have the knowledge, experience, or resources to assist them. Our networks are one of our most valuable possessions, and as they continue to expand and diversify, they become even more important to our business and personal lives.

The Tool

The tool could be anything that helps accelerate or "power up" your ability to accomplish your goals, and social media tools certainly fall into this category. Traditionally, when the old tool is "working just fine," we can be reluctant to embrace the new tool, despite its promise to be better, faster, or perhaps even cheaper. For instance, your old, paper address book (the tool) worked just fine, but you eventually made the switch to a new tool—perhaps Microsoft Outlook. The process of learning to use the new tool may have been challenging at first, but your commitment and persistence were rewarded when you finally figured out how to retrieve all that valuable information with the click of a button.

So, why did I take all this time to share with you my revelation about the Power Formula when I told you I would be teaching you about the capabilities and functions of LinkedIn? Because I want you to understand that the **unique experience** you have gained coupled with the **unique relationships** you have carefully developed gives you a tremendous advantage over the person who does understand **the tool** (in this case, LinkedIn) but is only beginning to gain experience and develop professional relationships.

Am I trying to discourage those of you who are younger business professionals or just starting your business careers? No way! This book will help you understand how to begin to develop your personal brand by creating a compelling LinkedIn profile and expand your network in order to accomplish your professional goals.

To help you keep focused on the Power Formula as you read this book, there will be a box at the end of each chapter that reemphasizes key points in terms of your **unique experience** and **unique relationships**. These sections will help you define your own power formula for succeeding in whatever you hope to accomplish in your career.

CHAPTER 2

The Million-Cubicle Project

LinkedIn—Making the Invisible Visible

On LinkedIn.com, you will find the following official definition: "LinkedIn is an interconnected network of experienced professionals from around the world, representing 170 industries and 200 countries. You can find, be introduced to and collaborate with qualified professionals that you need to work with to accomplish your goals." Let me start by addressing how LinkedIn works from a practical standpoint.

If you look at the page labeled Network Statistics, which you get to by clicking "Contacts" on the top toolbar and then clicking "Network Statistics" (see Figure 2.1), you will see that the page refers to your connections as "Your Network of Trusted Professionals" (see Figure 2.2). This is where LinkedIn differs significantly from social media sites like Facebook, where members attempt to get as many "friends" as they can—and where the word *friend* is loosely defined. With LinkedIn, the goal is to connect with only those people whom you consider to be trusted professionals. That leads to the first strategic decision you have to make: You need to personally decide whom you will consider a trusted professional based on the strategy you intend to pursue on LinkedIn. Some people choose to focus on expanding their networks even if this means embracing a loose definition of the word *trusted*. In contrast, I like to say a person is trusted if I can pick up the phone and ask him for a favor or an introduction and be confident that he would say "yes," or if he is someone for whom I would do the same.

Figure 2.1: Discover your Network Statistics page.

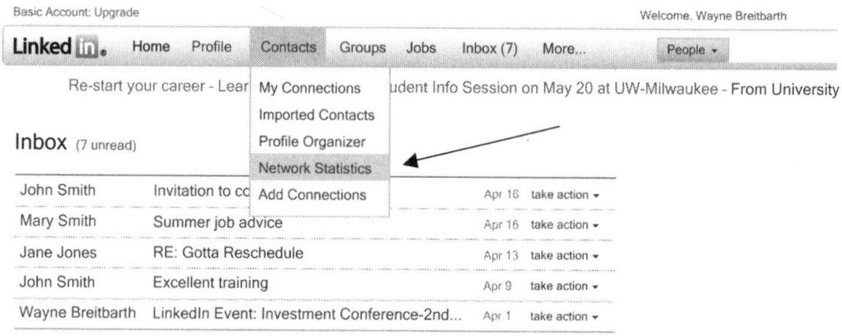

Figure 2.2: A network of trusted professionals is a valuable resource.

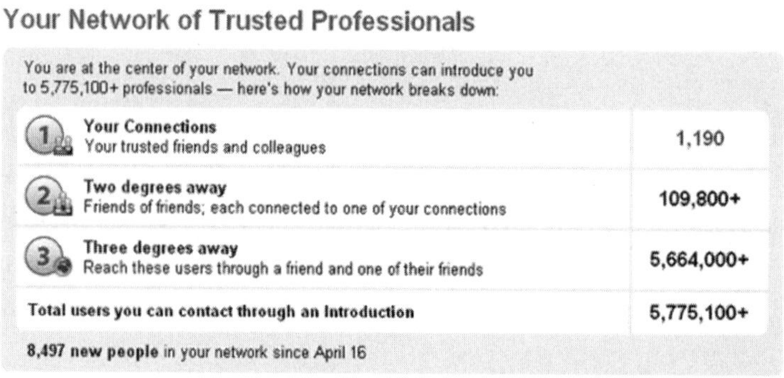

Your Network of Trusted Professionals

You are at the center of your network. Your connections can introduce you to 5,775,100+ professionals — here's how your network breaks down:

Your Connections Your trusted friends and colleagues	1,190
Two degrees away Friends of friends; each connected to one of your connections	109,800+
Three degrees away Reach these users through a friend and one of their friends	5,664,000+
Total users you can contact through an Introduction	5,775,100+

8,497 new people in your network since April 16

The person you just met in the vegetable aisle at your local grocery store typically does not meet my standard of a trusted professional. He might be a nice person and you may have enjoyed the two minutes of conversation, but that doesn't qualify him as "trusted" when he runs home and decides to look for you on LinkedIn. The decision about who is "trusted" is a very important starting point with LinkedIn, and there are lots of debates about this matter, but I personally stick with the definition I just described. I will provide additional comments and thoughts later on the always-raging debate between quality and quantity as it relates to your network.

We will now move farther down the Network Statistics screen (see Figure 2.3) and address degrees of separation—the Kevin Bacon concept that we are all connected by six degrees of separation or less to virtually everyone in the world. You will notice here that there are three circled numbers: 1, 2, and 3. The first group is one degree away from you; these are your personal connections, labeled with the subheading "Your trusted friends and colleagues."

Here is an example of how first-degree connections work. Let's say I have a friend named Joe Smith. Joe and I have been

Figure 2.3: LinkedIn makes your extended network visible.

Your Network of Trusted Professionals

You are at the center of your network. Your connections can introduce you to 5,775,100+ professionals — here's how your network breaks down:

1	**Your Connections** Your trusted friends and colleagues	1,190
2	**Two degrees away** Friends of friends; each connected to one of your connections	109,800+
3	**Three degrees away** Reach these users through a friend and one of their friends	5,664,000+
	Total users you can contact through an Introduction	5,775,100+

8,497 new people in your network since April 16

friends for a long time. Maybe we hung out in the rain at our kids' soccer games or perhaps we are close business associates. I decide that Joe and I should connect on LinkedIn. I search for his name, find him, and extend an invitation to Joe, asking him to join my LinkedIn network. Once Joe accepts my invitation, he does not need to turn around and invite me into his network as well. At that point, we are both connected to each other at the first level.

Your first-degree connections should be people who are already part of your offline network. You have a network that you have built over the course of your lifetime, whether that be high school, college, places you worked, clubs to which you belong, or acquaintances you have made in your day-to-day life. This is what I call your "flat" network. The premise of LinkedIn is that you transform your "flat" list of contacts into a dynamic, multidimensional network. Putting your contacts into LinkedIn will enable you to access additional degrees of depth within your network and will allow your contacts to assist you in new and valuable ways.

Let's go back to Joe Smith, my first-degree connection. If Joe were building a building and needed my products and services, he would probably call me because I know him so well. The fun begins when you think about the second degree. Let's say Joe Smith knows Bob Anderson. I have never met Bob Anderson. However, let's say that Bob is going to build a new building in town, and rumor has it that this building will contain over a million cubicles. As a furniture guy, a million-cubicle job in a town the size of mine would be a *really* big deal. Your equivalent of my million-cubicle sale might be finding the perfect job, meeting a strategic partner who will bring you additional revenue, finding a vendor that will enable you to decrease your production costs, or connecting with a foundation or individual who is interested in assisting your favorite charity.

Let's say I hear that Bob's company, The Anderson Company, is going to construct this building, and I put either "Bob Anderson" or "The Anderson Company" into the LinkedIn search engine and find out that my friend Joe Smith is connected to Bob Anderson. I find this out because when I do a search, I see that Bob's name is next to a "2nd" icon, which means he knows one of my Number 1 connections. I may know some of Joe's friends—having golfed, gone to parties, or hung out with many of them—but I definitely don't know all of them. For this example, let's assume that I do not know Bob and do not know how he knows my friend Joe.

So, learning of this connection after searching LinkedIn, I excitedly call Joe and ask him if he would connect me with his friend Bob Anderson, to which he replies, "Are you kidding? Of course. He's a good friend of mine. We've been friends for a long, long time. If my connecting you with Bob can help you, I'd love to do it." Isn't that what networks have always done? The added benefit of LinkedIn is that I can now see a list of Joe's connections and request an introduction to any of his connections I would like to meet.

Stop and think about the power of that. Without LinkedIn, what are the chances I would know that Joe Smith knows Bob Anderson? But with this tool, I can find it out almost immediately and can then use my network to connect with Bob.

Let's take it one step further, to the third degree, and imagine that Bob Anderson is friends with Jill Jones. Remember that I don't know Bob or Jill—I only know Joe. However, I now have the ability to search Jill Jones and The Jones Company, only to find out that Jill is building a building with—you guessed it—a million cubicles. I now have a chance to talk with her by contacting Joe, who contacts Bob, who contacts Jill.

Let's just take a look at the total number of people I have access to through LinkedIn (see Figure 2.4). Joe is a first-degree connection, Bob is a second-degree connection, and Jill is a third-degree

Figure 2.4: Your network grows exponentially.

Your Network of Trusted Professionals

You are at the center of your network. Your connections can introduce you to 5,775,100+ professionals — here's how your network breaks down:

1 Your Connections Your trusted friends and colleagues		1,190
2 Two degrees away Friends of friends; each connected to one of your connections		109,800+
3 Three degrees away Reach these users through a friend and one of their friends		5,664,000+
Total users you can contact through an Introduction		5,775,100+

8,497 new people in your network since April 16

connection, and I have 1,190 Joes, 109,800 Bobs, and over 5.6 million people in the Jill Jones category. These numbers never cease to amaze me. Sometimes I think there must be some dogs and cats in those numbers—there's no way I could be connected to that many businesspeople. However, I actually do have over 5.7 million human connections (no cats or dogs!), many of whom may just lead me to that million-cubicle sale. I have always had over 5.7 million people in my extended network; I just never knew who they were and how they were connected to me.

Remember the good old-fashioned method of networking? If I wanted to get ahold of either Bob Anderson or Jill Jones to talk about a potential business opportunity, I would be calling them (if I even knew their names) and sending e-mails, letters, postcards, whatever. The other thirteen furniture dealers who are located in my town would undoubtedly be using the same tactics. This would probably result in Bob and Jill screaming, "No more furniture guys!" With LinkedIn, I can have a friend or a friend of a friend assist me in making a contact that would typically be extremely difficult to coordinate. This is the number one power of LinkedIn: It takes connections that would normally be invisible and makes them visible.

Now let me give you an example of what could happen if you and your contacts choose to embrace the strategy of using a more casual definition of the word *trusted*. Say I am very excited about the opportunity of a cubicle sale because when I searched Bob Anderson and his company, I found that he is a second-degree connection. I call my first-degree connection, Joe Smith, and Joe says, "I don't think I know him. Who is Bob?"

"Bob Anderson," I say. "He is connected to you on LinkedIn. Of course you know him."

"Wayne, I really don't know him."

"You've got to be kidding me. He's a first-degree connection with you on LinkedIn. I can see it. How can you not know somebody in your network?"

If that happens several times, I might say to Joe, "Your network stinks. You really don't know anybody you're connected to. You just have a whole bunch of names in there, and you don't have any deep relationships with anyone. You're like a kid on Facebook."

That's why I stick with the premise that your network should be made up of people you know and trust; it allows you to help people. When you get to three degrees away, you hope the relationship that exists between yourself and your first-degree connection is as strong as the first to the second and the second to the third. If not, the connective power of LinkedIn can be greatly diminished.

The majority of books and blogs on the subject of networking say most business professionals have between 200 and 250 people they consider trusted professionals. If you're not on LinkedIn, these contacts are probably kept and managed in some kind of document or file, such as a Microsoft Outlook file on your computer, a card file, a list of names of people, a box of business cards in the top drawer of your desk, etc. All I am asking you to consider doing is taking those 200 to 250 contacts and getting them into LinkedIn. That way, you will not only have those 200 to 250 first-degree contacts; you will also gain the ability to know who their Number 1's and their Number 2's are. Your contacts' Number 1's and Number 2's then become your Number 2's and Number 3's. At this point, the number of people in your LinkedIn network can get incredibly large, as you saw in the previous example.

Let me stop and ask you this question: Can you have too many first-degree connections? If you answered yes, you are mostly correct. But let me ask the question differently: Can you have too many Number 1's as long as each one is trusted? The answer is no—as long as they are trusted, you cannot have too many first-degree connections, and you shouldn't second-guess the potential significance of what that Number 1 does, where he lives, or what his background is. That is not the point. As long as he fits your criterion of being trusted, make him a first-degree connection so that you can find out whom he is connected to—and potentially connect with all of his connections and his connections' connections. You have no idea who she plays golf with every Saturday or who he sat next to in church last Sunday.

In the past few years, I have read countless books, blogs, and commentaries about LinkedIn, and the quality versus quantity issue is continually debated by authors. This is the question of whether it's better to have a huge network of people you do not know very well or a smaller network of people with whom you are well acquainted. I consistently teach that your network should be made up primarily of trusted professionals. However, I do think there are certain circumstances in which you may decide to stretch that rule just a bit for strategic reasons.

One of those reasons could be that you are a recruiter, because recruiters are in the "body business." They need sizeable inventories of people with varied backgrounds and strengths; therefore, it makes sense for them to have very large networks. I actually heard about one international recruiter who has over 40,000 first-level connections. You may be in a similar situation that makes you decide to stretch the "trusted professional" rule. My feeling is that as long as you have thoroughly considered your decision, more power to you for using LinkedIn strategically.

I must admit that I occasionally stretch the definition of "trusted" myself. From time to time I invite people into my network even though I just met them the previous day at a networking event. This is typically the result of either having had an interesting conversation with the person or having reason to believe that further contact with him or her could lead to a mutually beneficial business relationship. Included with these immediate invitations will be a list of times I am available to meet for coffee or lunch so that we can continue to develop our relationship. These are what I call work-in-progress Number 1 connections. I work very hard at building these relationships to a point where I believe the person qualifies as a trusted professional.

As mentioned before, the real power of LinkedIn is that it takes connections that are normally invisible and makes them visible. Make your connections visible by transforming your "flat," offline network into a dynamic, multidimensional network of trusted professionals, and you will be on your way to securing that million-cubicle project.

APPLYING THE POWER FORMULA

- Your first step is to define what constitutes a trusted professional. I would suggest writing this definition down. These people make up that very important first part of the Power Formula: your **unique relationships.**

- If you are not sure whether to include someone as a contact, I would suggest you include him—as long as you do not consider him to be a competitive threat.

- Remember, with each new first-level connection you add, that person's Number 1's become new Number 2's in your network, and their Number 2's become new Number 3's in your network. That multiplication process helps you grow your **unique** network exponentially.

CHAPTER 3

Where's the Beef?

The LinkedIn Profile: Basics

Everyone starts on LinkedIn with a profile. A profile can be as simple as your name. However, if you choose to list little but your name, you will be missing a tremendous opportunity to avail yourself of the two major benefits of a LinkedIn profile: the ability to be found and the opportunity to tell your story.

Plain and simple, profiles should be beefy. For those readers who are old enough, think of the Wendy's commercial from the eighties in which the elderly ladies asked "Where's the beef?" as they looked at a tiny hamburger patty dwarfed by a massive bun. For those of you who are not familiar with the commercial, check it out on YouTube. You'll find it quite entertaining.

There are four reasons you want your profile to be beefy:

1. Your LinkedIn profile is a place where you can tell your story completely and fully, so that when people are

looking at your profile, they will be encouraged to do business with you over your competitors. They will see the depth and breadth of your experience, your professional recommendations, and the brands you carry, plus your certifications, educational experience, and all the other qualifications you possess that make you the obvious professional to do business with in the marketplace you serve. I like to refer to a LinkedIn profile as a "resume on steroids."

In contrast to a traditional resume, which is typically a listing of facts and dates, your LinkedIn profile allows you the opportunity to tell your story. It should be a narrative of sorts, where you emphasize your experience and high level of credibility. This "resume on steroids" should shout out "I'm the best at this in my market!"

To help tell your story, you can include details about yourself that, while perhaps bordering on personal information, will get across to the viewer who you are as a unique individual. For example, one of my class attendees told me that through the LinkedIn profile of a prospective client, he learned the guy collected wines—and he also found out which one was his favorite. On the day following his proposal presentation, he followed up with a thank-you note and included a bottle of—you guessed it—his prospective client's favorite wine, and the rest is history. He got the order.

2. Every word in your profile is keyword searchable. Thus, having a beefy profile will increase your chances of being found. As you know from using Google, keyword

searching on the Internet is an extremely powerful tool for finding people. Similarly, searching on LinkedIn can produce extremely valuable results. The search function enables you to find people who have certain types of experience, classifications, and/or brands. In subsequent chapters, I will address in detail how you can increase the likelihood of being found on LinkedIn by strategically including specific information and keywords in the various sections of your profile.

In a recent search, I was looking for a person interested in bicycling to join a group of cyclists for a charity event my company was sponsoring. Discovering a bicycling enthusiast who happens to be an architect or builder would be a home run. I would then be able to advance a professional relationship, help a charitable organization, *and* enjoy a day of bicycling. Therefore, I searched the words *builder, architect, cycling,* and *bicycling* and instantly had my choice of architects and builders with whom to spend the day. Without those keywords in their profiles, none of these people would have been found. The power of searching is discussed in detail in Chapter 10.

3. A beefy profile shows that you are not a dinosaur. What do I mean by this? For those of us in the Baby Boomer generation, people tend to appreciate the experience we possess, but they are also interested in knowing whether we are keeping abreast of the latest trends in the business world, including social media. A beefy profile will demonstrate that you are on top of current trends in your profession or

occupation and that you embrace technology. You are *not* a dinosaur.

4. You should expect your profile to regularly be compared with those of your competitors. Therefore, in order to gain a competitive advantage, you will want your profile to include a plethora of information, keywords, and details about who you are, what you hope to accomplish, and how you might be able to assist others.

Many savvy LinkedIn users will review a person's profile before meeting with her for the first time. Personally, I always look for common interests or discussion points before I jump into, "So, I hear you need some office furniture." Business professionals use their LinkedIn profiles to tell their stories. As a result, it can be extremely beneficial to review the profile of the potential customer, prospective employee, vendor, or other person with whom you desire to have a business relationship. Because of the vast amount of information available on the Internet in general and on LinkedIn in particular, it has become commonplace to "shop" several vendors online before engaging in direct communication.

Do yourself a favor and take a look at the profiles of some of your competitors. Observe what they are saying about themselves—awards they have won, certifications they hold, types of projects they have worked on, etc.—because this may jog your memory and remind you of similar information you could include in your profile. Based on the information contained in the profiles, would a potential customer be encouraged to do business with you as opposed to one of your competitors? If you think your competitor would get the nod, then start beefing up your profile.

Now that you know the reasons you want your profile to be beefy, the next several chapters will show you the steps to making sure you have all the necessary information on your profile. It's crucial that you complete your profile 100 percent as defined by LinkedIn. I am really a stickler on this, and it is not just because I am trained as a bean counter and like all the boxes checked. LinkedIn's research shows that you will be forty times more effective in your efforts on LinkedIn if you have a 100 percent complete profile. LinkedIn's definition of a 100 percent complete profile is as follows:

Name and Position:	25%
Picture:	5%
Summary:	5%
Specialties:	5%
Education:	15%
Past Job 1:	15%
Past Job 2:	15%
Recommendation 1:	5%
Recommendation 2:	5%
Recommendation 3:	5%

A 100% complete profile

Failing to complete your profile is akin to playing golf with a bag full of putters. Wouldn't you prefer to have fourteen different golf clubs in order to most effectively play that great game of golf? Make sure you use all the tools that LinkedIn offers; being forty

NANUET PUBLIC LIBRARY
149 Church Street
Nanuet, NY 10954
845-623-4281

times as effective is worth the effort of completing your profile 100 percent.

APPLYING THE POWER FORMULA

- It will be awfully hard for you to delegate the step of creating a beefy profile to someone else. No one knows your story like you do or can feel as passionate about why that story makes you the best at what you do. That passion will be evident if you personally craft a beefy profile that explains your **unique experience.**

- Try not to turn your profile into a bunch of marketing gobble-dygook. People want to read about what you have done in a simple, understandable format. You need to impress them with what you have accomplished, not with how many buzz-words you can include.

- Start to assemble the details of your **unique experience** by reviewing all of your past jobs and awards, but do not wait to get going on this until you think you have it all together. Subsequent additions to your profile are not only fine but preferable. I will address that topic in more detail later in this book.

CHAPTER 4

Your 30-Second Bumper Sticker

The LinkedIn Profile:
Personal Identification Box

At the very top of your LinkedIn profile is what I like to refer to as your personal identification box or, more descriptively, your 30-second bumper sticker. Like the physical business card you carry around and hand out to people the first time you meet them, this box identifies you with a few key pieces of information: your name, your headline, your photograph, your location, and your industry. This information (with the exception of your industry) travels around with you wherever you go on LinkedIn, whether you are participating in a discussion in the Groups or Answers section or whether you are connecting with new people. The elements of the identification box are very important; some people will never go to your profile to look at the details, but they will see your 30-second bumper sticker as you are active on Linked-In (see Figure 4.1). Let's address those components one at a time.

Figure 4.1: Create your own powerful 30-second bumper sticker.

Your Name

This element is pretty self-explanatory. Your name should include nothing but your full name, unless you have high-level academic degrees or easily recognizable certifications, such as PhD, MD, CPA, and certain other high-level insurance classifications or nursing classifications, etc. Personally, I wouldn't include designations on the level of an MBA.

Since there will undoubtedly be people who will only know them by their maiden names, some married women who have taken on their husband's last name find it useful to list a maiden name in parentheses. However, if you do not wish to list your maiden name or any other previous names in your headline, you can go to "Profile" on the top toolbar and choose "Edit Profile." Then click "Edit" next to your name and fill in the box labelled "Former/Maiden Name." Your former name will not be displayed, but listing it will allow people to find you if they search by the other name.

Your Photograph

I cannot stress the importance of the photograph enough. The photograph and recommendations are the two items that usually stop people from completing their profiles 100 percent. Most experts are in agreement on the importance of including a photograph, as well as the benefit of using a headshot (professionally taken or near professional quality) of yourself wearing business attire, smiling, and looking like a person with whom people would want to do business.

Let's talk about why personal photographs are a hang-up for some people, especially members of the Baby Boomer generation. Plain and simple, we Baby Boomers are afraid to admit that we are in our fifties or sixties. Well, the reality is that you cannot hide behind the computer screen and pretend you are twenty-eight years old forever, and you surely are not going to be able to hide your age when you show up for the job interview or when you show up to collect the check for the order the customer placed after you found him on LinkedIn and put together the sale. So get over it!

Many times people will remember a face before they remember a name. I want to be the person people find on LinkedIn the day after they meet me at an event and say, "I really liked that bald furniture guy. That's the guy. I recognize him by his picture." The person who recognizes you from your photo may be the one who leads you to your million-cubicle sale.

Your Headline

A basic headline consists of the company you work for and the position you hold there, but the headline field can contain 120 characters, and it is your opportunity to tell an abbreviated version of your story. In it, you will want to describe your experience and mention how you can help someone who sees your 30-second bumper sticker. Clicking "Edit" next to your current headline allows you to edit the information in the box titled Professional Headline.

For the first seven or eight months I was on LinkedIn, my headline read, "President and Owner, M&M Office Interiors, where we give you the space you want and the experience you deserve, and LinkedIn trainer." "The space you want and the experience you deserve" is the tagline for the company I own. I love my tagline. I paid a lot of money for my tagline. It was the result of very extensive research, and I definitely think it stands for the brand we have in the marketplace. However, as much as I love my tagline and what it says, it does not clearly state that my number-one priority is selling office furniture. My headline now reads, "President, M&M Office Interiors, where we have served the office furniture market for over 50 yrs, and LinkedIn Trainer." It doesn't incorporate my business's tagline, but it better describes me as a business professional. Unless you work for a multinational corporation that is a household name, you cannot assume that readers of your profile will know what type of products or services you provide. It is imperative for your headline to clearly express what your company does and/or what your business proposition is.

If you have multiple jobs or a primary job and a secondary job, be sure to list all positions you hold. My primary position is president of M&M Office Interiors, but I also provide LinkedIn training, and thus I have listed both positions as part of my headline. If you are looking for a job, your headline should clearly state that you are a job seeker looking for a position as an IT professional in the food manufacturing/distribution business, for example. If you do not enter a customized headline, LinkedIn will use your most recent job title and company name as your descriptive headline. But do take time to create a powerful headline; it could be the deciding factor in someone's choice to connect with you or look at the details in your full profile.

I personally prefer a narrative-type headline, but a popular alternative is a style that consists of keywords separated by the pipe symbol. To get the pipe symbol, use the shift key together with the backslash key. Some people choose this option because LinkedIn's current search ranking formula gives extra weight to the words in your headline. Because you only have 120 characters available for your headline, using the pipe symbol will allow you to put more keywords in your headline. Using the pipe symbol, my headline might look something like this:

Haworth Office Furniture Dealership President | LinkedIn Trainer, Speaker, Consultant & Author | Social Media Consultant

Whichever option you choose, include your most important keywords, so that when people search for the keywords you included, they will find you—and not your competitor who didn't think to put keywords in his headline.

Your Location and Industry

The final component of your personal identification box is the location and industry in which you do business. LinkedIn will assign you a region based on the zip code you provide, but you will need to manually select your industry from the list LinkedIn provides. The industries currently offered by LinkedIn are not very specific in some cases, but they are adding more all the time. For example, "office furniture" is not on the list at this time. Since my company provides interior design services, I could select "design." However, I have chosen "furniture" because I feel that more accurately describes our industry. On a regular basis, I check to see if LinkedIn has added a category that more precisely describes the services we provide. I suggest you do the same if your specific industry is not on the current list.

In summary, I cannot overemphasize the importance of your personal identification box. It will travel with you and be your identifier throughout LinkedIn. Be sure it is thorough and correct. If you do not have a photograph or a complete headline, you may cause someone to question your credibility or fail to thoroughly understand your business. As a result, he or she may choose to do business with someone else. Follow the steps I have outlined, and you will be on your way not only to a great 30-second bumper sticker but also to a terrific LinkedIn profile.

APPLYING THE POWER FORMULA

- Your goal with the headline is to create a compelling marketing statement about your **unique experience** in just 120 characters, while also including some critical keywords. Create a few drafts of your statement, and then ask several of your closest connections for a critique of what you have written.

- Do not use an outdated photo of yourself. You are attempting to demonstrate your **unique experience**, and experience comes with age. People need to see you in that photo and put that picture together with the person they just met or are going to meet.

CHAPTER 5

Resume on Steroids

The LinkedIn Profile: Experience Section

As mentioned earlier, I like to think of the LinkedIn profile as a "resume on steroids," and the section of your profile that most resembles a traditional resume is the Experience section. You will find this section toward the bottom of your profile, and the information in your Experience section is also summarized within the top box. In my summary in the top box (see Figure 5.1), you will notice that I have listed every job I have had since I graduated from college.

People often ask me what jobs they should put on their profiles. These are the criteria I suggest you use, not only for jobs but for anything else on your profile:

1. Does putting this on my profile add to my story or increase my credibility?

2. Does putting this on my profile make it easier for people to find me?

3. If I do not put this on my profile and my competitors have it on their profiles, will I be at a competitive disadvantage? In other words, will I be mad I didn't include it on mine?

Figure 5.1: An effective Experience section includes all jobs and volunteer activities.

Current	
	• Office Furniture Dealership President & Owner (Preferred Haworth Office Furniture Dealer) at M&M Office Interiors [Edit]
	• Founder & Linkedin Trainer at Power Formula [Edit]
	• Board Member & Volunteer Instructor at Make A Difference-Wisconsin [Edit]
	• Board Member at The Community Warehouse [Edit]
	• Volunteer High School Mentor at Urban Promise Lunch Club [Edit]
	see less...
	✚ Add Current Position
Past	
	• Volunteer Youth Leader at Eastbrook Church
	• Executive Vice President at Russ Darrow Automotive Group
	• Vice President at Heiser Automotive Group
	• Manager Small Business Division at Arthur Andersen & Co
	see less...

If the answer to any of these three questions is yes, then, by all means, include the position on your profile.

My recommendation is to put every job you have ever held on your profile. Describe them in detail—the position you held, what you accomplished, and what experience you gained—and include a list of awards you received while you held each job. Use plenty of relevant keywords. You will want to highlight not only your present area of expertise but also any specialties relating to previous positions. This is important because when someone searches LinkedIn for a professional with experience in multiple disciplines, the combination of keywords will increase your chances of being found.

It is very important to spend plenty of time crafting the job descriptions on your profile. All too often people fail to spend sufficient time on this because the detail of the Experience section shows up so far down the page, and they are tired or anxious to move on to other tasks. Do not make this mistake. You never know which job experience or accomplishment will put you ahead of the other candidates in the eyes of a potential customer or employer. And if certain keywords show up multiple times on your profile because you use them in multiple job descriptions, you will be listed higher in the search results, which is definitely a good thing.

You will also notice that on my profile I have listed several volunteer positions, both present and past. Viewers of my profile can see that I am actively involved in giving back to my community, and most of us like to hire and work with people who care about others. This is another way to impress viewers of your profile prior to a face-to-face meeting or telephone call. For job seekers, listing volunteer positions and relevant extracurricular experience is a must. For new graduates, where actual job experience may be in short supply, this is your way of showing potential employers that you have been actively involved with specific organizations, worked as part of a team, held leadership positions, and contributed to your community.

Another reason for listing all jobs you have held is that recommendations must be attached to a job or education entry; a person cannot post a general recommendation to your profile. Therefore, every job listing gives you another opportunity to include an enthusiastic recommendation from a trusted colleague or professor, previous employer, or satisfied customer.

Though it is actually not part of the Experience section, let me mention one of LinkedIn's recent additions to the Profile section.

Immediately following your experience entries, you now have the opportunity to list skills, publications, certifications, patents, and other languages you speak. Entries in this section will certainly increase your credibility as well as supplement and/or expand upon the information you shared in your Experience section.

The Experience section is an extremely important component of your "resume on steroids." Spend a significant amount of time writing a detailed description for all jobs listed—remember, your beefiness in this area will help you tell the story of who you are as a professional and will give you many chances to use keywords.

APPLYING THE POWER FORMULA

- In order to be sure that each entry you make on your profile thoroughly explains your **unique experience**, try to think of each job as if it were the only one you ever had. This will help you get very detailed in terms of experience, accomplishments, awards, responsibilities, etc. Sometimes we tend to cut corners because, in total, the profile looks fine. However, you never know which of those details presented in a job listing will resonate with the reader of your profile or be the important keywords that help someone find you.

CHAPTER 6

Aren't You Any Good?

The LinkedIn Profile: Recommendations

Recommendations are a critical element of your profile for the following reasons:

1. The number of recommendations you have received is highlighted in the top box of your profile page and when your name appears in a listing of group members.
2. The number of recommendations you have is one of the weighting criteria in ranking search results on LinkedIn.
3. Recommendations are the only outside verification of the information you have provided on your profile.
4. Words included in the recommendations are keyword searchable.

For these reasons, it is imperative that you get recommendations. I urge you—please, please, please, do not skip this important element of your profile. Spend time on it. Particularly if you are a job seeker, *do not* skip this part. It is one of the major things you will have going for you when it comes to the credibility of your profile.

If you are hesitant to go about getting recommendations, let me ask you this question: Aren't you any good? Of course you are. You, like most experienced businesspeople, have undoubtedly established a great reputation in your marketplace relating to the goods and/or services you provide. By working hard to get LinkedIn recommendations, you are simply documenting your great reputation so that people who review your profile will understand who you are and what you stand for, which is sure to result in improved business opportunities in the future.

Before he or she can post a LinkedIn recommendation on your profile, the person writing it must have a LinkedIn account and be connected to you. Therefore, if you have an important connection who is not on LinkedIn but who may be willing to write a LinkedIn recommendation for you, you might have to take some time to show him why he should be on LinkedIn, help him set up his profile, and then ask for the recommendation. You will be doing him a tremendous favor, and at the same time he will be helping you.

I know soliciting recommendations is hard work, but let me put this important step in perspective by comparing it to a game called Jenga, where wooden blocks are stacked to form a tower. Players take turns removing blocks from the tower, progressively weakening its stability, until an integral block is removed, causing the tower to fall. Think of the tower as a 100 percent complete profile and the individual blocks as the elements of your profile. Your tower may continue to stand without the recommendation block, the photograph block, or some other block. However, at some point your tower will become unstable, and you'll realize that your LinkedIn efforts weren't as effective as they could have been if you had completed your profile 100 percent. Get those three recommendations that are necessary to have a 100 percent complete profile. Playing with a full set of Jenga blocks will make you a winner at the LinkedIn game.

How Many Recommendations Should I Have?

I recommend that you seek out two or three recommendations for every job you have ever had. You should also seek out two or three recommendations for any work you have done with nonprofit organizations and for each educational experience, especially if you are a young business professional or in job-seeking mode. The number of recommendations you have received is included in the top box, and some people assume that the more recommendations you have, the better you are at what you do. So get busy and secure those recommendations, bearing in mind that quality is as important as quantity.

You can have too many recommendations. I have actually seen people with upwards of 200, and I believe that is too many—your profile becomes way too long and people could begin to lose interest.

What Should My Recommendations Say?

Recommendations should be specific and strategic, and you should attempt to get them from the most influential people willing to comment on each position you have held. Assist the person writing the recommendation by reminding her of some of the accomplishments, skills, or specific things you brought to the workplace. Many people are willing to write a recommendation but need to be reminded of your noteworthy accomplishments. Sending them a list of specific achievements and helpful keywords will not only make the task of writing a recommendation less time-consuming but may also result in a more accurate and effective recommendation.

Here is an example of a well-written recommendation I received from a person who attended one of my LinkedIn classes:

"Wayne facilitated a LinkedIn training session for the UWM School of Continuing Education. His information was practical and immediately applicable—I came back from the training and updated my profile and applied several of his other tips right away. Just as beneficial as his training sessions are the wonderful tips he sends via e-mail to those who choose to receive them. Today's tip on saving my contacts and profile took just a couple of minutes and could potentially save me a large amount of time and frustration should something ever happen to my profile. Furthermore, Wayne is more than willing to go above and beyond to help educate others on using LinkedIn as an effective tool, which is why I am so excited to have him be a part of an upcoming social media workshop in Washington County. But most importantly, Wayne's passion for helping people, whether it be in training LinkedIn, choosing the right office furniture, or in any of the various volunteer organizations of which he is a member, is so evident and contagious. Thanks, Wayne, for sharing your passion and knowledge!"

Why Are Recommendations So Important?

The first reason recommendations are so important is that they complete your profile and get you to 100 percent. Second, and more important, they are the only item on your profile that you do not personally write. As with most information on the Internet, profiles are only as trustworthy as the people who create them. Recommendations are the only outside verification of the information you have provided on your LinkedIn profile. I have had several people tell me that recommendations in their profile were a very significant factor in their ability to land the perfect job. In many cases, the hiring executive told them so.

Recommendations are also important because if a person writes a recommendation for you, your name and the fact that she recommended you will appear on her profile. It's really cool to think about your name popping up on some else's profile, especially if she is a person of influence.

Tips for Getting Recommendations

So now you're probably thinking, *Where am I going to get all those recommendations? People don't do those anymore. I don't even know where my ex-boss is!* Do not overlook the fact that you can get recommendations from people besides your direct superior, such as a person who worked above your superior or the owner of the company. You could also ask a supplier or vendor for a recommendation. A customer with whom you have had an exceptionally strong relationship may be willing to write one for you. Last but not least are coworkers who can verify the specific points you want to emphasize about your background, experience, and work ethic.

As I mentioned previously, recommendations can also be posted in reference to educational experiences. I encourage you to search out these recommendations, especially if you are a younger business professional—and preferably before you graduate. Most professors consider it a privilege to assist a good student in securing his first job out of college.

One way to get recommendations is to give recommendations. If you write a recommendation for someone and she posts it to her profile, LinkedIn will automatically ask her if she would like to write a recommendation for you. I am not a fan of exchanging recommendations when it simply becomes friends endorsing friends. "He's a really good guy" is simply not a recommendation worth having, and sometimes these reciprocal recommendations consist of little more than that. However, if a recommendation exchange fits a specific need or situation, remind the person you are recommending that she could return the favor with her own detailed, specific, and strategic recommendation of you.

Prior to posting a recommendation to your profile, it is acceptable to suggest that the writer make revisions or corrections. LinkedIn gives you a chance to review a recommendation and send it back to the writer to request that any errors be corrected or that additional details or keywords be added. Generally, the person who has written a recommendation for you will be more than happy to accommodate your suggestions.

Let me give you one final tip. If you want to have a great Monday morning, sit down on Sunday and write three or four recommendations for other people, totally out of the blue. If you do this, I am confident that no later than midmorning on Monday you will receive e-mails, phone calls, and comments through

LinkedIn thanking you for writing a recommendation. People will say, "I can't believe you took the time to do that for me!" I have done this, and it works. The reason it sets you up for such a nice Monday morning is that it gives you a wave of confidence; you'll be ready to take on the day. Try it. You will have a lot of happy friends and connections going forward.

I want to close this chapter with a thought-provoking question: How would you feel if your competitors had more significant, specific recommendations on their profiles than you have on yours, and do you think those recommendations might make a difference as a potential customer or client reviews both of your profiles?

Case closed!

APPLYING THE POWER FORMULA

- You will be surprised by how much your **unique** connections would love to help you document and explain your **unique experience** by composing a well-written recommendation for you. Just ask!

- If you think of recommendations as a power booster for the **unique experience** part of the Power Formula, you will be more diligent in getting this part done. And believe me—it's definitely a power booster.

- Differentiation from competitors is easy when you get a significant number of well-written recommendations.

- An added benefit of receiving recommendations is that the writer's name and company name appear in your profile. That sounds like a boost to your **unique experience** to me. Your name will also appear on the writer's profile—power boost times two!

CHAPTER 7

Hyperlinks to Hot Leads

The LinkedIn Profile: Additional Top Box Items

In this chapter I will cover the remaining items included in the top box—the box outlined in blue at the top of your LinkedIn profile.

Education

I recommend that you list all the education you have had, including high school, college, and any significant additional education you received that relates to your industry and/or specialty. One of the benefits of listing all your educational background is that when you are looking to add lots of connections in a hurry—which we will discuss in a subsequent chapter—LinkedIn helps you use the schools or other institutions you attended as a way of finding people with whom you might like to connect. People sometimes ask me why I would want to list my high school. The first reason is the one I just gave you: It can help people find you. The second reason is that people tend to like to do business with fellow alumni, whether they are from high school or college. You cannot predict why a person might select you over your competitors, but a common educational experience could be the deciding factor. So, do yourself a favor and list all schools you have attended.

Under each educational entry, include specific information regarding what your degrees required and what credibility you have because of those degrees. This could include specific classes, internships, leadership roles, study abroad experiences, or anything else you feel shows that your educational experience was more comprehensive than simply completing the coursework required to receive a degree or certification. This is another great way to add credibility to each and every entry on your profile. You can also list significant industry-specific classes, workshops, or seminars you have attended by going to your profile, clicking "Add Education," and selecting "Other" instead of an option from the list LinkedIn provides. You can then type in whatever information about that opportunity you feel will enhance your credibility (see Figure 7.1). An added benefit

Figure 7.1: Enhance your credibility by highlighting nontraditional educational experiences.

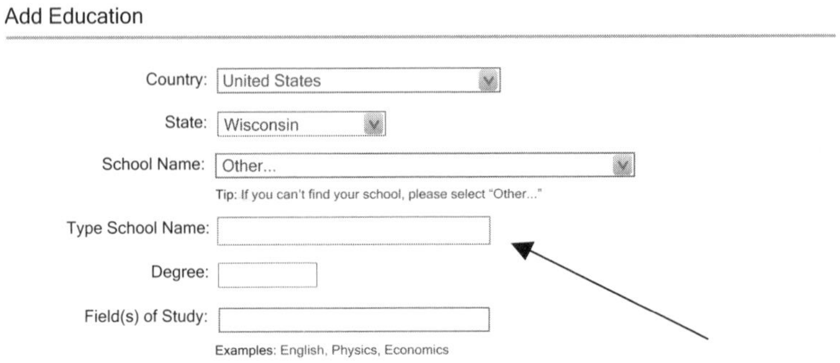

Add Education

Country: United States
State: Wisconsin
School Name: Other...
Tip: If you can't find your school, please select "Other..."
Type School Name:
Degree:
Field(s) of Study:
Examples: English, Physics, Economics

to listing every educational experience is, of course, the opportunity to receive recommendations for each of these entries.

Websites

The next section of the top box is Websites, which contains hyperlinks to places in which you have a web presence (see Figure 7.2). People typically have only one thing listed here, most often the website of the company they work for, and the link is usually titled "My Company." Your company's website is a good place to start, but there is a lot of marketing opportunity going to waste if you stop there. You can designate up to three links, and this is the only place in your profile where you are allowed to have a direct link to other places on the Internet. Linking enables you to direct people to wherever you would like them to go, giving you the opportunity to send people not only to your company website but also to, for example, a signup sheet where they can get on your mailing list. You can link to videos, on YouTube or elsewhere on the web, and you can link to other social media sites like Facebook, your blog, etc.

Figure 7.2: Move your reader to action by listing three critical websites.

Education	• Marquette University • University of Wisconsin-Whitewater • Dodgeland High School <div align="right">see all...</div>
Recommended	40 people have recommended you
Connections	500+ connections
Websites	• M&M Experience You Deserve [Edit] • Beginning Linkedin Training [Edit] • Haworth Adaptable Bldg Video [Edit]
Twitter	• WayneBreitbarth [Edit]
Public Profile	http://www.linkedin.com/in/waynebreitbarth [Edit]

Websites is also a great place to display additional areas of interest, such as organizations and charities in which you are involved, and you will be promoting these organizations' websites by adding them to your profile. You have lots of flexibility here, and you *do not* have to list the URL of your LinkedIn profile as one of the three sites. Using all three for links to other websites will also move your LinkedIn profile up in the search results of sites like Google, Bing, and the other search engines.

Be sure to describe each of these websites. Most people don't realize they have this option and go with the default of "My Company" or "My Blog." In reality, you can describe your websites with up to twenty-six characters. Don't miss this opportunity to brand these websites and give one more little marketing push about what you do and what you stand for. You can alter the website's description by selecting "Other" in the pull-down menu and then typing the new description in the box next to the link (see Figure 7.3).

Figure 7.3: Creative website descriptions will encourage readers to take a look at your websites.

Public Profile URL

When you join LinkedIn, you in effect create your own one-page website—your LinkedIn profile. If you look at Figure 7.4, you will see an example of a URL LinkedIn automatically assigned to a profile. Notice that it includes the user's name and several other seemingly random characters. LinkedIn does, however, allow you to assign your profile a more descriptive URL, and most people choose to simply add their name after www.LinkedIn.com/in/ (see Figure 7.5). I'm lucky to have a unique name that no one had claimed yet, but when you click the Edit button next to your public profile URL, you may find that your name has been taken. If that's the case, you can add a middle initial or a number following your name in order to save the URL. Changing this address to something closer to your actual name allows you to use the URL on your resume, letterhead, and/or business card so that people can easily access your profile—your "resume on steroids."

This brings up a point you should understand: When you build a personal LinkedIn profile, you automatically create a public profile, which can be seen by anyone on the Internet who visits your URL. However, you can control exactly how much information is in the public domain, which I refer to as the "Google world," and how much you share only with the LinkedIn community. If you have a photograph on your LinkedIn profile, you can choose to omit the

Figure 7.4: Your initial public profile URL includes random numbers and characters.

Education	• University of Wisconsin-Madison - School of Business
Connections	1 connection
Public Profile	http://www.linkedin.com/pub/dave-johnson/8/216/119

Figure 7.5: A personalized LinkedIn URL will enhance your marketing and branding efforts.

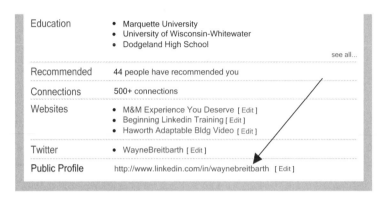

Education	• Marquette University • University of Wisconsin-Whitewater • Dodgeland High School
	see all...
Recommended	44 people have recommended you
Connections	500+ connections
Websites	• M&M Experience You Deserve [Edit] • Beginning Linkedin Training [Edit] • Haworth Adaptable Bldg Video [Edit]
Twitter	• WayneBreitbarth [Edit]
Public Profile	http://www.linkedin.com/in/waynebreitbarth [Edit]

picture from your public profile so that people searching on Google cannot see it. When people are searching on Google or other search engines, your public LinkedIn profile will typically come up on the first page—hopefully it is the very first thing that shows up—but it does not need to have all the same content as your LinkedIn profile.

I choose to put everything that I have on my LinkedIn profile on my public profile. I keep my profile very professional, and I want all that information to be in the Google world. That way, if a person is not on LinkedIn, he can still see all the pertinent information about me, all the experiences I have had, all the recommendations I have received, and so on. You'll have to decide how much of this information you want to have available in the Google world, and if you stick with a very businesslike LinkedIn profile, you should be able to put almost everything on your public profile as well.

There are certain things I do not put on my profile at all. I don't list my home address, phone numbers, birthdate, names of my children and where they went to high school, my wife's name—those kinds of things. All those items can be put on LinkedIn, many of them in boxes at the bottom of your profile.

Whether you do so is your call. My decision is to avoid including that information—again, so I can feel comfortable putting my whole LinkedIn profile out in the Google world.

The items that complete your top box—education, websites, and public profile URL—are crucial to enhancing your credibility and improving the functionality of your LinkedIn profile. Don't lose energy and neglect to fill them in just because you're getting close to the bottom of your profile. They are all things that could make you stand out as better than the other guy. Be sure to spend the time and effort to craft them carefully and thoughtfully.

APPLYING THE POWER FORMULA

- Do not downplay or forget to include the details of your educational entries; they are an important descriptor of your **unique experience.** With 2,000 characters per job or educational entry, you have a lot of space to use. Remember, integrating keywords into your profile is part of the goal here as well.

- Your current company's website should be your first entry in the Websites section. This will add to the description of your **unique experience**—especially if the website includes customer profiles, a company history, descriptions of what your company does, etc.

- I cannot emphasize enough the importance of including industry-specific workshops, certifications, and training courses as key components of your **unique experience**. It just takes a few moments, and there's a really good chance that your competitors have missed this opportunity, despite the fact that they may have the same experience. This can be a great differentiator.

CHAPTER 8

That's My Boy!

The LinkedIn Profile:
Summary and Specialties Sections

This chapter will concentrate on the most important section of your LinkedIn profile outside of the top box: the section right below the top box labeled "Summary." Within that box is a sub-heading, "Specialties," which is also extremely important. I have analyzed hundreds of profiles, and I continue to be amazed by how underutilized these two sections are; they can be so powerful in explaining your personal and business brand to viewers of your profile. The keywords included in them can also be very beneficial in helping people find you.

The Summary Section

I like to think of this section as your cover letter, because in it you address the reader just as you would in a traditional cover letter.

You can also use the summary to direct people to other sections of your profile and emphasize or summarize information you have detailed elsewhere.

The Summary section can contain up to 2,000 characters, and I recommend taking full advantage of every available character. If you write this section in narrative format, I suggest you use first person, as if you were talking directly to the person reading your profile. Another option is to compose the section in a concise, bulleted format. My preference is for the narrative format because it allows you to write as you would speak, giving the section a conversational feel. If you do write the Summary section in narrative format, consider the specific items you need to cover and the major topics you want to address. You may have several businesses and/or interests you want to highlight in this section of your profile, but this isn't a place to list every detail of every job you've ever had. Save that information for each respective job description in the Experience section, where you get 2,000 characters for every job. You can summarize some of your work experience in this section, but it is best to use your first paragraph to outline what you are trying to accomplish as a professional, who your perfect customer is, or other information that will help the reader relate to you. After reading the first paragraph of your summary, you want the reader to say, "I'd love to meet this person."

If you are a job seeker, this section should start off with a few sentences outlining the types of jobs that would be a perfect fit for your knowledge and skills. The remainder of the summary should describe why your experience has led you to that conclusion. Include details about how you have saved your previous employers money or increased productivity. You should explain these achievements in the Experience section, but you should also briefly highlight them here as well; some people may not make it down to the detailed job description, and this will be your only chance to tell them about that achievement. If you are a job seeker who is changing career paths, this is the place to explain why you have decided to make a change after years in a different industry or company.

These are some of the topics you may want to include in this section, depending on what your strategy is:

- A brief summary of the types of job experiences you have had
- Highlights of specific (hopefully quantifiable) things you have accomplished
- An excerpt from a letter of recommendation or testimonial, especially if you have not been able to obtain a LinkedIn recommendation from the person who wrote it
- Some of your hobbies or interests and why they make you a desirable employee or business partner
- Steps the reader can take to get further information on some of your accomplishments, projects you have completed, or awards you have won
- Why it is that you think your experiences make you qualified for this next career step
- A brief description of any business relationships that have brought about superior results
- New markets you are considering going into and how viewers of your profile might fit into your plan

My LinkedIn Summary Section

Here is my LinkedIn summary, which will hopefully demonstrate the concepts discussed:

I am the proud owner and president of M&M Office Interiors, a full-service interiors provider with products and services that include commercial office furniture, raised floors (TecCrete), moveable walls, carpeting, interior design, space planning, project management, and installation and delivery of office furniture. We are the exclusive distributor of Haworth office furniture and architectural interiors products in southeastern Wisconsin. You can view a video by clicking "Haworth Adaptable Building Video" in the website section above. M&M has been providing office furniture solutions to the southeastern Wisconsin marketplace for almost 50 years. We have the area's largest office furniture showroom, with over 11,000 square feet of display area. So, when you bring your team in to "check it out," you can "test drive" products in a very unique environment. We are located at W233 N2833 Roundy Circle West, Suite 100, Pewaukee, WI 53072.

****

I am also very passionate about training people on the business social networking platform LinkedIn. I have trained thousands of busy businesspeople on how to effectively use LinkedIn in my two classes: "LinkedIn Power Formula Training for Beginners" and "Intermediate LinkedIn Power Formula Training."

Click on the link in the website section above to see the details of my upcoming beginner's LinkedIn class. I also provide weekly LinkedIn tips that are received by thousands of subscribers for FREE. Let me know if you want to be on that list. If you are unable to attend one of my live LinkedIn classes, I have 90-minute DVDs for sale of my beginning and intermediate LinkedIn classes. Contact me for details on how you can get a copy of these very informative videos. In the SlideShare section below, you can watch a short promotional video of what you can expect to see and learn at my live LinkedIn classes as well as on my DVDs.

As you can see from my Summary section, you can break up this section with a row of dashes, stars, or dots. This indicates to the reader that these are separate and distinct endeavors. This section should be written so that if your mother read it, she would say, "That's my boy!" Make sure this "cover letter" section of your profile will be clearly understood by most people and that it is not loaded with gobbledygook or jargon. Yes, you still need to be very conscious of the keywords that will put you in the search results you want to be in, but also be sure your story is well-told and that the reader can clearly see the experiences and accomplishments that got you where you are in your career.

Since LinkedIn does not have a built-in spell-check, write this section in Microsoft Word or another word processor, do a spell-check, count the number of characters (remember that LinkedIn only allows 2,000), and then paste the contents of that document into LinkedIn, confident that your mother will be proud.

Specialties

Below the Summary heading is a subheading, "Specialties." I like to think of the Specialties section as your pantry full of keywords. In my Specialties section, I begin by discussing some of the brands I work with and giving specific information I would like people to know about me, but then I complete the section with a comprehensive list of the keywords I want to be searched by. This is another way to ensure that your name will come up as people search for topics relevant to what you do. Do not hesitate to repeat some of the keywords you included in the Summary section; using those keywords multiple times will move you up in the search rankings. As you list these keywords, be consistent with the identifiers you use in other materials—like company brochures, websites, and business cards—so that there is consistency between all those marketing vehicles and your LinkedIn profile.

My LinkedIn Specialties Section

Here is what I've listed in my Specialties section. Notice that I included a frequent misspelling of my last name, which ensures I'll be found even if someone makes this common mistake.

> M&M Office Interiors represents more than 200 manufacturers, including Haworth (exclusive), Office Furniture USA (OFUSA), OFS, Lacasse, HON, Paoli, and many others. I am also very involved in LinkedIn, networking, social media, & business development. KEYWORDS: Office furniture, Haworth, interior design, Wisconsin, Milwaukee, LinkedIn, Christian, accountant, CPA, interiors, furniture, raised floors, moveable walls, social media, trainer, teacher, instructor, Brietbarth, LinkedIn Power Formula.

If you are a company owner, make sure all your employees who are on LinkedIn use the same type of wording when describing the company and its history and accomplishments. It is very important for a company to present a consistent, keyword-searchable message throughout the LinkedIn universe.

You may find it beneficial to review the Summary and Specialties sections put forth by some of your competitors. Seeing how they state their business proposition may assist you in thinking about how your business is different from theirs. Remember, none of us has cornered the market on being the only smart guy on LinkedIn. Learn from the profiles of your competitors—that is one of the beauties of LinkedIn.

As I close this chapter, I want to emphasize an important point that applies to your entire profile but tends to crop up most often as people write their own Summary and Specialties sections: You must be willing to brag about yourself when documenting your accomplishments and experiences on your profile. If you have trouble doing this, have someone else help you describe why you are the perfect person for the job or why you should be the vendor of choice. Remember this, too—your competitors will undoubtedly have no trouble bustin' their buttons with pride, so you'd better not be shy about bustin' yours.

APPLYING THE POWER FORMULA

- "Talk to me." That is the phrase I want you to keep top of mind as you write your Summary section. This is one of the few parts of your profile where you have a blank space and no specific boxes to fill in as you share the story of your **unique experience**.

- Take your current marketing materials (brochures, websites, handouts, etc.) and identify all the brands you represent. Be sure they are all included in your Specialties section. If your proposition is **unique**—for example, if you are the only person in your region representing a particular brand—make sure the person viewing your profile knows this by including this information in your Summary section.

- If you have **unique**, important terms that are often mis-spelled, consider including the misspelled form. That way, when someone searches by that misspelled word, you will still be found.

CHAPTER 9

Not Your Average Joe

The LinkedIn Profile:
Must-Have Applications and Tools

Throughout the previous chapters on LinkedIn profiles, I have consistently emphasized the fact that one of the major purposes of your profile is to show credibility. Your profile and your actions on LinkedIn should establish you as an expert and prove that you are not your Average Joe. This chapter will discuss applications that will make your profile unique and comprehensive, as well as another tool—LinkedIn Answers—that is an excellent way to build that all-important credibility.

Late in 2008, LinkedIn introduced profile applications, additional tools that reside on your profile and add functionality to LinkedIn. Although there are many applications, there are a few I feel can be especially instrumental in helping you show credibility. In my opinion, the must-have LinkedIn applications are:

1. Box.net files
2. Google Presentation or SlideShare
3. Reading List by Amazon
4. Events

You can access these applications by going to "More" on the toolbar at the top of the LinkedIn page and then clicking "Get More Applications." From there, simply select the ones you want to attach to your profile.

Box.net Files

Box.net files allow you to post PDF, Excel, or Word files to your profile. These files can then be downloaded by visitors. This is a great place for you to post white papers, articles, company brochures, pictures of your projects or products, customer testimonials, and other documents that increase your credibility and helpfulness (see Figure 9.1). Job seekers can post PDFs of their resumes (minus whatever information they do not feel comfortable displaying, such as address or phone numbers) or letters of recommendation from people who are not on LinkedIn.

Let me give you an example of how I have successfully used Box.net files. The very first Box.net file I have on my profile is titled "Checklist for Moving Your Office." When I meet a person at a networking event who is moving offices, right after I quit salivating about a potential sale, I hand him my business card and say, "Check out my LinkedIn profile—the very first item in my Box.net files is a checklist for moving your office. Print it off and give it to the person responsible for the move. He or she will simply love the checklist." This gives me immediate credibility and displays my expert status and my willingness to help. When that person goes home from the event and downloads the file, he will think, *Boy, Wayne has already added value in a brand new relationship. I think I'll continue this relationship and call him for help with the move and furniture for the new office.* LinkedIn will notify me when this download has taken place, which is helpful in following up with this potential customer.

Figure 9.1: Use Box.net files to share helpful information and increase your credibility.

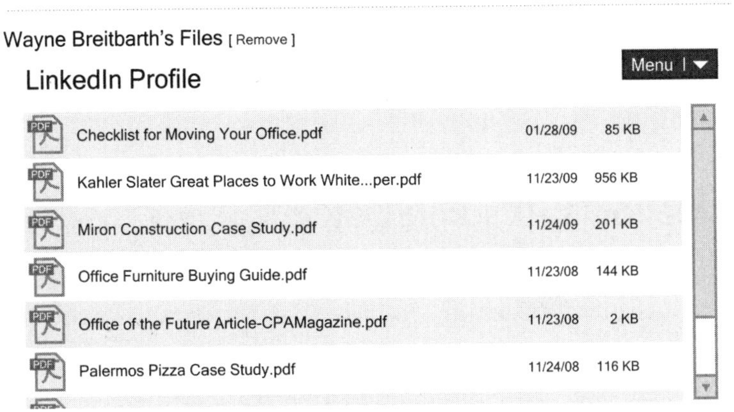

Wayne Breitbarth's Files [Remove]

LinkedIn Profile

Menu | ▼

PDF	Checklist for Moving Your Office.pdf	01/28/09	85 KB
PDF	Kahler Slater Great Places to Work White...per.pdf	11/23/09	956 KB
PDF	Miron Construction Case Study.pdf	11/24/09	201 KB
PDF	Office Furniture Buying Guide.pdf	11/23/08	144 KB
PDF	Office of the Future Article-CPAMagazine.pdf	11/23/08	2 KB
PDF	Palermos Pizza Case Study.pdf	11/24/08	116 KB

Google Presentation / SlideShare

These two applications allow you to post slide shows (Power-Point or otherwise) of presentations that showcase your personal expertise, presentations about your company, and/or pictures of projects you have done (see Figure 9.2). Video is becoming an increasingly important part of many companies' branding efforts, and if video is part of your slide show, you can post those files here with the YouTube downloader. (Remember that you can also link to video in the Website section of the top box.)

Figure 9.2: Use PowerPoint presentations to share your expertise with others.

Amazon's Reading List
======================

Many businesspeople tend to be readers, but even businesspeople who aren't avid readers like to talk about books. Amazon's Reading List application is not only a helpful way to suggest books to people and bring content and color to your profile; it also enhances your credibility and displays your interests to viewers (see Figure 9.3). With Reading List, you can select books you have read, and then the book's cover and your review and rating will show up on your profile. It's like being a book critic on your own profile. In addition to allowing other people to follow the books you're reading and how you rate them, the application also allows you to follow other people's reading lists, which makes for a great conversation starter the next time you see them. Like many other applications, when you post an update or a new book to Reading List, LinkedIn sends out a notice to your entire network. Your first-degree connections not only benefit from the information you are sharing, but your name is brought to their mind, which is always a good thing. It may even remind them to give you a call about that million-cubicle job they heard about last week while working out at the gym.

Figure 9.3: Use the Amazon Reading List to share your diverse interests with others.

ReadingList

A Million Miles in a Thousand Years: What I Learned While Editing My Life
by Donald Miller
See this book on Amazon >
Wayne has read this book

👍 Recommended

Comment: "If you liked Blue Like Jazz, you will love this. If you haven't read Blue Like Jazz you should but..."
Read more >

Me 2.0: Build a Powerful Brand to Achieve Career Success
by Dan Schawbel
See this book on Amazon >

The last two books you reviewed on your Amazon Reading List show up right on your profile. To view your entire book list, visitors have to click through to the application. My suggestion is that your two most recently reviewed books always include one book that shows your expertise in your business area and one book that relates to a personal interest, which will show another side of you to the viewer of your profile. I know people look at the books I post on my profile because they often mention them when conversing with me at events I attend. The Amazon Reading List quickly identifies common interests and is just another opportunity to connect with someone on a personal level.

Feel free to hone your review-writing skills by writing a rockin' review of *The Power Formula for LinkedIn Success* and including it in your profile. If you would like some public exposure, you can post your review in the Customer Reviews section on the book's Amazon.com listing.

Events

The Events application is a powerful networking tool, but many people do not recognize its strategic value. There are a few quirks in how it works—including that it was down for almost a week with no notice or explanation—but it's still a great application, especially for you power networkers. It is also helpful for job seekers; you can use it to find events to attend and other opportunities to get out and meet the person who is going to lead you to that next position.

What can the Events application do for you?

1. It is a great way to publicize your events to your connections and the entire LinkedIn network.
2. Your event is completely searchable by keywords in the event description, tags (defined by the event organizer) that describe the event, and the title of individuals who should consider attending. It is hard to believe this is free.
3. You get to keep track of who is going to events with the RSVP function. This enables you to identify whether someone you are anxious to meet is scheduled to attend a specific event.
4. If you say you are attending an event, it shows up on your profile and in the network updates of all the people you're connected to, once again putting your name, face, and

headline in front of your connections (see Figure 9.4). The event stays on your profile until the date has passed.

5. You can search events you might want to attend by industry or location. This is particularly beneficial when you are out of town and searching for productive activities in the place you're visiting.

Figure 9.4: Why attend an event alone when you can use the Events application to encourage others to join you?

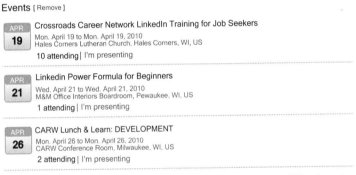

Events [Remove]

APR 19 Crossroads Career Network LinkedIn Training for Job Seekers
Mon. April 19 to Mon. April 19, 2010
Hales Corners Lutheran Church, Hales Corners, WI, US
10 attending | I'm presenting

APR 21 Linkedin Power Formula for Beginners
Wed. April 21 to Wed. April 21, 2010
M&M Office Interiors Boardroom, Pewaukee, WI, US
1 attending | I'm presenting

APR 26 CARW Lunch & Learn: DEVELOPMENT
Mon. April 26 to Mon. April 26, 2010
CARW Conference Room, Milwaukee, WI, US
2 attending | I'm presenting

See all Wayne's events >

Be sure to review all the LinkedIn applications to see if they might be helpful in increasing your profile's credibility and appearance. There will undoubtedly be more applications added as this type of interface becomes more and more popular. Take advantage of these.

Despite the fact that up until now I have described the elements of the user profile in their default LinkedIn order (Top Box, Summary, Specialties, etc.), you can rearrange these sections and any applications. Because some readers may never read the middle or bottom portion of your profile, you may find it advantageous to place your most important information near the top. For example, if you feel that moving your applications up would tell your story more effectively—especially because you have some excellent new slide shows and PDF files—do it. If you are a student who has little in the way of job experience but very substantial and impressive educational entries, you may want to move those entries up above Summary and Specialties, or at least above Experience and your applications. You will see an arrow cluster to the left of each section of your profile. To rearrange the sections, simply drag the arrow cluster to the desired location (see Figure 9.5).

Figure 9.5: Strategic placement of your profile components can greatly improve your effectiveness.

✤ Recommended By   ✦ Get Recommended

Office Furniture Dealership President & Owner (Preferred Haworth Office Furniture Dealer) at M&M Office Interiors

22 visible recommendations, 2 new recommendations for this position: [Edit]

"I just returned from one of Wayne's LinkedIn classes, and have to say he is the LinkedIn master. For starters, he really knows the in's and out's of how to get the most out of all LinkedIn's tools for each person. I've been on LinkedIn since 2005, and I learned many new functions from him. But most important, he explains the WHY and STRATEGY behind using LinkedIn to truly be effective. Finally, it really doesn't hurt that Wayne is an incredibly talented and entertaining presenter. If you haven't seen him yet, you need to!" *June 29, 2010*

Giving (and Getting) Answers

LinkedIn Answers is a feature that—like the above applications—gives you an opportunity to share your unique knowledge and make your LinkedIn presence more dynamic. You get to this part of LinkedIn by selecting "More" on the top toolbar and then choosing "Answers."

The Answers function enables you to use your own knowledge to answer questions posed by other people. This can prove to be quite useful if you are looking to gain regional or national exposure as an expert on a certain topic. From the Answers page, you can browse topics related to your industry or expertise—they're listed on the right side of the page under "Browse." You can also search by keyword to find relevant questions. Giving thought-out, knowledgeable feedback to other LinkedIn users is an excellent method of building your credibility and providing value to the community.

You can attempt to secure an answer from a specific part of your network, all of your network, or the entire LinkedIn universe. When you request an answer from your network, it will go to those individuals in the form of a LinkedIn message, and thus they can respond to you privately as opposed to posting a public answer on the LinkedIn site. You can also direct your inquiry to people in your network who meet certain criteria or have a particular expertise. For example, if you have a question about interest rates, you may want to direct your inquiry to the bankers in your network. When you pose a question to all of LinkedIn, you will have to put your question in a specific category (administration, law and legal, financial markets, nonprofit, etc.), and you will receive answers from people all over the world.

Maximizing your use of the applications and tools discussed in this chapter will allow people to identify your areas of expertise and witness your desire to help others, which will significantly enhance your credibility. This is your chance to prove that you are *not* your Average Joe.

APPLYING THE POWER FORMULA

- How better to explain your **unique experience** than a PowerPoint presentation or video that positions you or your company as experts in your field?

- Be sure to use Box.net files for posting customer testimonials. Posting testimonial videos using SlideShare or Google Presentation might be even more effective.

- Every time you read an industry-related book, be sure to include your expert comments on the Amazon Reading List application for increased credibility.

- When people say they are either attending or interested in attending an event you have posted using the Events application, their names show up on the RSVP list. This is a great way to showcase your **unique relationships**.

CHAPTER 10

Who Do You Want to Find?
Searching on LinkedIn

There are two major uses of LinkedIn, and we have spent a significant amount of time discussing the first use: being found. I have shown you how to develop a very beefy profile, which will allow you to be found based on keywords and the story you have told. In this chapter I will address the other major use of LinkedIn: finding others. LinkedIn can be used for finding not only prospective customers and clients but also for finding:

- New strategic vendor and supplier relationships
- People you want to join you in a project or endeavor, including a charity or not-for-profit with which you are involved
- New employees
- An expert in a specific industry
- Someone you want to engage in a social/business event (e.g., a golf outing or networking event)

- People you want to meet when you are out of town for an event
- A speaker for an upcoming event you are hosting
- People who are responsible for organizing events at which you may be qualified to speak or participate

By using keywords and other search criteria—such as region, job title, group affiliation, etc.—you can easily find the people you are looking for. Ask yourself, *Who do I really want to find?* As a business owner, business developer, or job seeker, you will need to identify which keywords the person you want to find has most likely included in his profile. If that person has done a good job of creating his profile, it will include those keywords.

Bear in mind that by the time this book hits the shelves, Linked-In will have around 100 million members. In other words, once you select your search criteria and hit the Search button, you are looking through what is the largest database of resumes in the world. No tool like this existed prior to LinkedIn, and the site becomes more and more useful each time a new person joins—and someone signs up every second of the day. As LinkedIn becomes increasingly popular, the database will become that much more useful. But enough of the generalities—let's get on to how an actual search might work for you.

I am always thinking about the keywords my potential customers would have in their profiles. Two of those words would be *facility* and *facilities*, because in many of the larger corporations the people I target have titles like Director of Facilities, Facility Manager, or something of a similar nature. I do most of my searching in the Advanced People Search function of LinkedIn. If you go to the top of any LinkedIn page, you can access this by clicking the word "Advanced," which is just to the right of the magnifying anuet Public Library

Title: Trump : how to get rich
Item ID: 32824010172836
Date charged: 8/3/2019,12:43
Date due: 9/3/2019,23:59

Title: LinkedIn for Dummies
Item ID: 32824011365165
Date charged: 8/3/2019,12:43
Date due: 8/17/2019,23:59

Title: The power formula for LinkedIn succ
ess : kick-sta
Item ID: 32824010607823
Date charged: 8/3/2019,12:43
Date due: 9/3/2019,23:59

Questions? Call 845-623-4281

Figure 10.1: Use the top toolbar to access the Advanced People Search function.

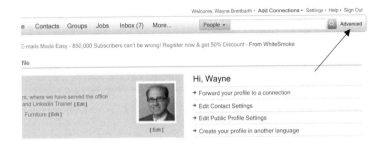

glass on the top right of the toolbar (see Figure 10.1). I type "facility OR facilities" in the keyword box and push the blue Search button at the bottom of the screen (read more about the "or" search function on page 102). This searches the entire LinkedIn network for my query, ultimately finding 75,818 profiles that have the word *facility* or *facilities* in them (see Figure 10.2). That's obviously too many for me to review, and my market is not the entire world. So, if I go back and modify the advanced search to find contacts within a 50-mile radius of my zip code, I now get 764 results (see Figure 10.3). That number is much more manageable and more regionally relevant, and if you think about what it

Figure 10.2: A broad-ranging Advanced People Search may provide an impractical number of results.

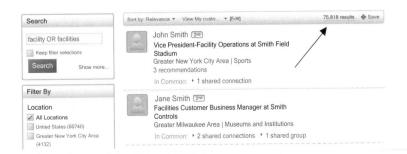

Figure 10.3: Add more specific criteria to narrow your search.

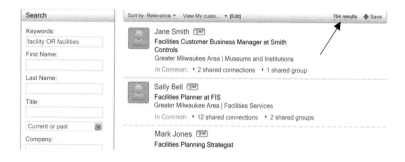

represents—people in my region who somewhere in their profile have the word *facility* or *facilities*—you see that it's an important list for me.

But let's continue refining the search before we look at the profiles. Let's say that, on top of *facility* or *facilities*, I would like to search for employees of a certain company. So, I choose one of the larger companies in my marketplace, Harley-Davidson, and add it to the Company line (see Figure 10.4). Now I am searching for Harley-Davidson employees with *facility* or *facilities* in their

Figure 10.4: Further refine your search to uncover your perfect targets.

profiles who work at a location within 50 miles of my zip code. That produces 13 results.

By now I think you see how you can use the different search boxes on the Advanced People Search page, which allows you to narrow the entire LinkedIn database down to a small, targeted group.

I want to stop for a moment and talk about how the size of your network affects the results you receive when searching on LinkedIn. People come up to me regularly and say, "I've been to your class and I can't get LinkedIn to work. I'm just not finding anyone." The first question I ask them is "How many connections do you have?" When they proudly tell me they have 35 connections, I tell them they are fishing for muskie with a minnow net.

I am an avid fisherman, and in Wisconsin the grandpappy of all game fish is the muskie. When my wife and I are fishing for muskie, we place a huge net in the middle of the boat, always ready to net "the big one" once we get it close enough to the boat. You need that huge net if you want to catch a trophy-size muskie. The LinkedIn equivalent of the muskie net is a significant number of connections. There is no exact number you must have to perform effective searches, but I do know it takes at least 50 to 70 quality connections before your search will consistently "net" you significant results (no pun intended!).

Let me ask you this question: If one of my competitors decides to search for facilities people working at Harley-Davidson in the Milwaukee area and she has 35 connections, how many people from her network will appear in the search results, bearing in mind I came up with 13 and I have 1,190 first-level connections? If you said zero or one, you are probably right. This part of LinkedIn, the finding part, really rewards the person who has spent time building his flat network and then makes the effort to put those people into LinkedIn as first-level connections. As discussed earlier in the book, the ongoing process of adding connections will always pay off; each time you add a Number 1, you are adding Number 2's and Number 3's who might work in facilities at Harley-Davidson. However, do not lose sight of the fact that I am still talking about having a quality network of trusted professionals. You do not want to lower the quality bar merely to increase the quantity of your connections.

Saved Searches

Once you land on a search that produces quality targets for you, LinkedIn allows you to save that search. This is one of the best features on LinkedIn, but it is often overlooked. From the screen that shows your search results, simply click "Save" on the top right and then choose whether you want LinkedIn to send you an e-mail weekly or monthly to notify you if a new person who meets your search criteria has been found in your network (including Levels 1, 2, 3, and Groups). You can save up to three searches with a free LinkedIn account.

If you are not saying to yourself, *Oh my gosh, that is so cool!* you are not understanding the power of the saved search function. This is a perpetual lead generator, and it is absolutely free. So, when LinkedIn notifies you of a new search result, get on the phone and set up a meeting with this person who has become a part of your network. It could turn out to be a home run.

In response to user surveys that I conduct on a semiannual basis, Advanced People Search is consistently rated as the most useful feature on LinkedIn. This is really where the money is. It's where you will undoubtedly see the majority of your productivity on LinkedIn. Once your network has grown to "muskie size" and you have learned how to maximize your search results, you should begin to see an even greater return on your time investment in LinkedIn. Using the all-important keywords, consistently try to identify and search for the person you would love to find and make a connection with—and then get the net ready.

APPLYING THE POWER FORMULA

- The winner in the searching part of the LinkedIn game is the person who has the most **unique relationships** (in other words, connections). It's as simple as that.

- My research shows that, on average, for each **unique relationship** you have included in your first level on LinkedIn, you will have approximately 100 additional Number 2's and 4,700 Number 3's. Now that's what I call leveraging your **unique relationships**.

- Saved searches is your way of making sure that LinkedIn is looking for your future **unique relationships** 24/7, even when you are sleeping, on vacation, or hanging out with friends.

CHAPTER 11

I Found You—Now What Do I Do with You?

Contacting the Person You Just Found

You will remember that we found a list of facilities people at Harley-Davidson in the Milwaukee area that consisted of 13 connections. Figure 11.1 shows the names of some of those people. Now you need to review the profile of each individual and make sure that person is someone you would actually like to meet. If you decide to proceed at this point using the good old-fashioned business techniques we have used for years, like picking up the phone, e-mailing, etc., at least you now know the name of the person and are not simply cold-calling Harley-Davidson and asking for the facilities person. But if you have no success with the traditional methods, you can pull up his LinkedIn profile and scroll down the right-hand side, where you'll see who in your network knows that person (see Figure 11.2).

Figure 11.1: Narrow your search further by reviewing profiles.

Last Name:			Shane Smith [2nd]
Title:			Area Manager - Aluminum Machining and Powder Coat at Harley-Davidson
			Greater Milwaukee Area	Automotive
Current or past ▾			In Common: ▸ 1 shared connection
Company:			Donald Smith [2nd]
harley davidson			Plant Engineer at Harley-Davidson
Current ▾			Greater Milwaukee Area	Automotive
School:			In Common: ▸ 1 shared connection ▸ 1 shared group
Location:			Thomas Roberts [2nd]
Located in or near: ▾			Enterprise Asset Management professional
Country:			Greater Milwaukee Area	Automotive
			9 recommendations

Figure 11.2: The invisible has just become visible.

entation of EAM strategies in manufacturing environments.

How you're connected to Thomas

ntenance and Reliability

npany
oyees; Automotive industry
2 months)

You
⇩
William Jones
⇩
[2nd] Thomas Roberts

jy for Maintenance and Reliability Operations in alighment with
'rovide the guidance and direction to insure predictability, stability
of all maintenance processes, Establish direction and execution of
maintenance process.
ses to understand critical business functions that need to be

Thomas Recommends (10)

Tim Johnson, *Plant Manager, Harley-Davidson Motor Company*

(i.e. purchasing, production, engineering, finance or human
rements which will maintain or improve business performance
to identify key performance indicators which will be monitored to
int of business performance.

❝ Tim's intellect and leadership ability sets him...

Scott Mathews, *Financial Analyst, Harley-Davidson Motor Company*

This is where you could pick up the phone, call your friend, and ask how strong a relationship he has with the person at Harley. If your friend's network is made up of trusted professionals, you could request that he make an introduction or pass along a message to the Harley employee to give your efforts to connect with that person a bit of a push. Isn't this what people in your network have always done for you? The difference with LinkedIn is you can now know who knows whom by simply pushing the Search button. As I stated earlier, this is one of the great powers of LinkedIn; it makes connections that are normally invisible visible.

The Introduction Function

LinkedIn's Introduction function can help you get introduced to a second- or third-level connection. This tool allows you to draft a LinkedIn message to the second- or third-level connection you want to meet, send it to your first-level connection, and then ask him to pass it along to his first-level connection. You can access the Introduction function in one of two ways. If you know the name of the person you want to meet, you can click "Get introduced" from the search screen (see Figure 11.3). If you are viewing the person's profile, you can click "Get introduced through a connection" (see Figure 11.4). You can do this with either a second- or third-degree connection, but the second-degree connection will be easier since it only requires connecting through one friend. A third degree requires your friend to pass your message on to a person you do not know, who then passes it along to the person you want to meet.

Figure 11.3: Initiate an introduction via LinkedIn.

If you click on "Get introduced through a connection" and you are connected to your ultimate target through more than one person, you will need to select which of your first-level connections you feel will be in a better position to help you. Once you select that first-level connection, you will then get a screen that looks like Figure 11.5. There will be two boxes—one for the message to the person with whom you would like to connect and another for the message to the person you know and trust. In the message to the person you want to meet, simply explain your business proposition and why you would like to meet, no differently than if you were picking up the phone. In the box for your friend, start with a personal greeting, and then ask him if he would pass the introduction along through LinkedIn.

Figure 11.4: Get introduced after viewing an intriguing profile.

When you push the Send button, those two messages go to your trusted connection, and this is where some of the power of LinkedIn comes in. Your connection gets a chance to write something nice about you, maybe even about the project or product you talked about in the message, and reaffirm that you are a good person to work with. Then, when he pushes "Send," that information goes on to the person you wish to meet.

Figure 11.5 : Your connection's endorsement may open the door.

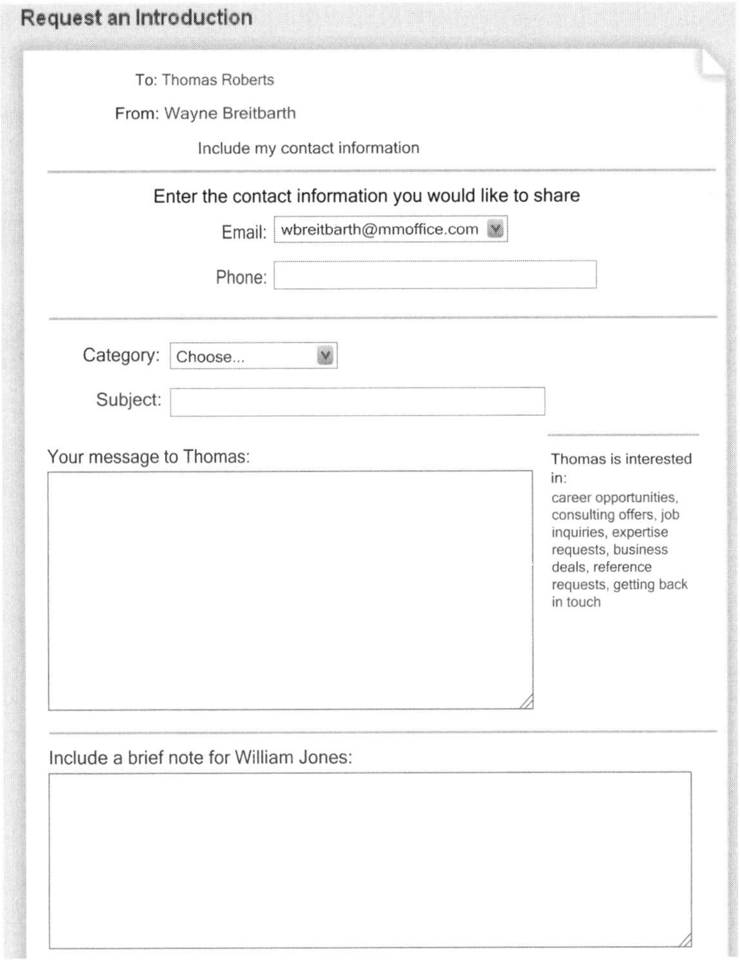

Request an Introduction

To: Thomas Roberts

From: Wayne Breitbarth

Include my contact information

Enter the contact information you would like to share

Email: wbreitbarth@mmoffice.com

Phone:

Category: Choose...

Subject:

Your message to Thomas:

Thomas is interested in:
career opportunities, consulting offers, job inquiries, expertise requests, business deals, reference requests, getting back in touch

Include a brief note for William Jones:

You should know that the very first time you attempt to use the "Get introduced through a connection" function, it may feel a little odd, since most of us did not grow up connecting through the Internet and social media. We grew up using things like the telephone, regular mail, and, most recently, e-mail for making connections like this. But soon I suspect the Facebook generation will see social media as the primary way to connect with people. Remember, this generation barely recognizes that they can pick up the telephone and have a real-time conversation.

Even if you are comfortable with meeting a new contact through LinkedIn, you will need to make sure your friend understands how the Introduction function works and what his role in the process is. With a free LinkedIn account, you can have only five outstanding introductions at any given point in time, so you want to be sure that none of them get stuck with someone who is unfamiliar with LinkedIn introductions. If your friend hasn't passed on the introduction after several days, you may need to call him up and explain the process.

You can see the progress of your introductions no matter what step they are in. If you are trying to connect with a third-degree connection, you will not know who the connection between your first-level connection and the third-level connection is, but you will still be able to see the status of your message when it is with him or her. Even though requesting introductions to third-level connections adds an extra step, remember that your pool of potential contacts gets much larger when you include these third-level connections—and it sure beats cold-calling a total stranger.

In my opinion, using the Introduction function on LinkedIn is a more respectful and potentially more effective way to ask for an introduction than using the telephone. With the Introduction tool, your connection gets a chance to review your message when he has sufficient time to do so; you don't have to tie him down and ask for an introduction while he is busy trying to get work done. He also gets the chance to write a detailed recommendation about you to pass along to his friend, and if he does so, the connection is much more likely to take place. For these reasons, I think LinkedIn's Introduction feature will be a tool that many people will come to use more frequently, especially as more members of the Facebook generation join the workforce.

No matter which technique you decide to use—phone, snail mail, e-mail, face-to-face, or the LinkedIn Introduction tool—the information you receive after doing an advanced LinkedIn search will help you get to the person you want to meet much faster and more effectively than any tool we've had up to this point in our business careers.

APPLYING THE POWER FORMULA

- When you write a message to the person you want to meet, be sure to highlight or reaffirm your **unique experience** and explain how that experience will help your target accomplish his or her goals.

- If you are the individual passing along the introduction to a connection, help your friend out by saying something nice about him and his capabilities so that your connection is encouraged to reach out.

CHAPTER 12

There's Gold in Them Thar Hills
Expanding Your Network

As you can tell from previous chapters, the winner of the searching aspect of the LinkedIn game is the person who has a lot of connections. However, please continue to keep in mind my recommendation that you only add to your network people whom you know and trust, because when you add a new contact, you put your extremely valuable network in his or her hands. Remember, it is **your** network. It is a possession you have worked your entire career to build, and when you add a connection on LinkedIn, it is like handing your Outlook database to that individual and trusting him to treat it professionally as you would treat his.

I recommend you have an ultimate goal of acquiring at least 200 to 250 connections (muskie size), as opposed to the 20 or 30 connections (minnow size) that the vast majority of LinkedIn users acquire. If you want your searches to be useful, you really want to consistently add connections. This chapter will show you how to find new people to add, accept or decline the requests you'll get, and gather interesting information about your expanding base of contacts. Once you've built your muskie-sized net, when you go fishing, you'll be sure to come up with lots of potentially valuable connections.

The most common way to add connections is one at a time. You do this by clicking "Add Connections" on the top toolbar (see Figure 12.1). All you need is the person's e-mail address, and then you can use LinkedIn's standard invitation to invite your friend or colleague to join your network

The preferable way, however, to add a person to your network is to search for her by name and then click "Add [her name] to your network" at the top right corner of her profile. Once you make this selection, you must then tell LinkedIn and the person how you know her by selecting one of the options LinkedIn shows you: colleague, classmate, etc. I prefer this method of adding connections rather than the option mentioned in the previous paragraph because it allows you to enter a short personal note explaining why it would be beneficial for the person to allow you to be part of her network. In my opinion, the standard "I'd like to add you to my professional network on LinkedIn" is very lame.

Figure 12.1: Adding connections one at a time is as easy as 1-2-3.

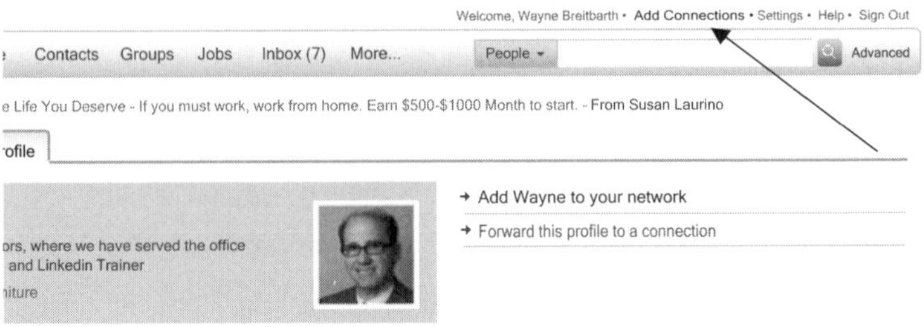

Remember, you are adding this person to your group of trusted professionals. Therefore, you should add a personal touch to your invitation. Customizing the connection request will get you a much higher response rate.

Now I am going to show you how to add a lot of connections at the same time. Even if you're starting out with no contacts, you should be able to get to 50 or 60 connections within three or four days by following the four steps that follow. If you currently have 30 or 40 connections and follow these steps, you should get to over 100.

Importing Contacts

The first step is to import contacts (see Figure 12.2). Click "Contacts" on the top toolbar. Then select "Imported Contacts." At that point LinkedIn will be searching your entire database for contacts. It searches Outlook by default, but it can do any other database or e-mail account, including ACT, GoldMine, Yahoo, Gmail, or even a simple Excel file with name and e-mail. LinkedIn will sift through the entries in your database, looking for e-mail addresses that match those of people who are on LinkedIn. When

Figure 12.2: Press the button and relax while LinkedIn finds connections for you.

it's done searching, you will see the screen shown in Figure 12.3. What you're looking for is the little blue square that says "in." That icon indicates the contacts in your database who are already on LinkedIn. What do you think the odds are that they will want to connect with you once you send them an invitation? Probably close to 100 percent.

Check the boxes next to the names of the contacts you want to connect with and click the button labeled "Invite selected contacts." This will send a group invitation to the people you have selected, and you will have to be fairly creative in crafting your personalized message, since it is going to many different people. You could do something like this:

Hi. I just read a great book by Wayne Breitbarth on LinkedIn, and I finally understand how powerful this thing is. I would love to have you join my network.

—John Doe

Figure 12.3: Quickly connect with trusted professionals who are already using LinkedIn.

Connecting with Colleagues

The second step to building your network is adding colleagues. Click "Add Connections" on the top right toolbar, and then click on "Colleagues" (see Figure 12.4). LinkedIn will then take all the jobs you have included in your profile and create a comprehensive list of the people on LinkedIn who were employed at those companies during your tenure (another benefit to listing all jobs you have had). If you perform this same search at a later time, the list will include only people who have been added since the last time you searched.

Figure 12.4: Past and present colleagues can be extremely valuable connections.

Connecting with Classmates

The third step, connection with classmates, is fun—it will feel like you're on Facebook. Click "Classmates" (see Figure 12.5). Select a school and the years you attended that school, and LinkedIn will give you a list of all the people who said they attended this school during the years you indicated. You will probably get quite a large number of potential connections, but if you say to yourself, *Well, that's too many; that's going to take me too long to review*, then I guess you don't really understand why you are even on LinkedIn. Rather than viewing this process as a hassle, treat your search for valuable connections as if you were hunting treasure—tell yourself, *There's gold in them thar hills*. Your classmates present a tremendous opportunity to make some important connections. These are people who will remember you from your college days, and you will now be able to tell them what you are up to today. Reconnecting with old friends is fun, but it can also be very productive; some of your old drinking buddies may now be presidents of the companies with which you are trying to do business. Many others will likely have nice databases of Number 1 connections, which could lead to great connections at the second or third level for you. You just never know.

Figure 12.5: Connecting with a classmate may lead to that million-cubicle deal.

The Outlook Toolbar

The fourth step is downloading the Outlook toolbar, which you can get by clicking on "Tools" at the bottom of any LinkedIn page. Click "Download it now" in the Outlook Toolbar box (see Figure 12.6). This will download a piece of software to your computer, which, going forward, will search all the e-mails you receive for contacts who are in the LinkedIn database. The program will also tell you when people you have in your Outlook database join LinkedIn. In addition, when you are writing an e-mail to a new contact in Outlook, a pop-up box will tell you whether the recipient is a LinkedIn member and how many connections he currently has—and it will give you the option to add the person as a LinkedIn connection.

Figure 12.6: The Outlook Toolbar—your virtual assistant—looks for potential connections 24/7.

Choose one or all of LinkedIn's productivity tools
Search, build your network, and manage your contacts, all from the applications you use today.

Outlook Toolbar ◄	Browser Toolbar
Quickly and easily build your network using Outlook	**Quickly search and access LinkedIn anytime**
✔ Build your network from frequent contacts	✔ Quick search from anywhere
✔ Manage your LinkedIn contacts in Outlook	✔ Direct access to LinkedIn
✔ Stay connected to your network	✔ See your inside connections at any hiring con
Learn more Download it now	Learn more

"People You May Know"

On your LinkedIn home page, you'll see a box on the right labeled "People You May Know" (see Figure 12.7). LinkedIn has a special formula for putting people in this section, and although they have not revealed how it works, you will be amazed at the names you find here. From my observation, these people typically fall into one or more of the following categories:

- They are connected to someone in your network.
- They attended a school that you also attended.
- They are a member of a group to which you belong.

Figure 12.7: LinkedIn helps you find new connections.

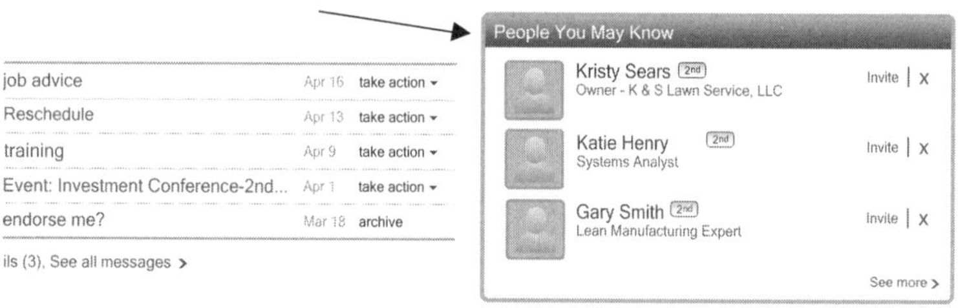

You will find these suggestions not only useful but also somewhat entertaining. LinkedIn has helped me find a number of guys I used to drink dime taps (10¢ beers) with during my college days! Do not overlook the usefulness of this feature in finding new connections.

Accepting or Declining Connection Requests

People frequently ask me what they should do when somebody they don't know invites them to connect on LinkedIn. This will begin to happen with greater frequency as you become more active on LinkedIn, especially if you decide to join larger groups. Some people assume that because you are members of the same group, you will want to connect with them on the first-degree level.

When you receive an invitation from someone, you will see the screen in Figure 12.8. Let's go through the six options you have when responding to an invitation:

1. **Accept**. The person will immediately become a first-degree connection.

2. **Reply**. People often overlook the option of using the Reply feature. If you hit the Reply arrow, you can send a communication to the requesting individual without allowing him to become part of your network. If I have had an interesting meeting with a person and we belong to the same group or club, I can send a message saying something like, "At the next meeting, let's make sure we connect and get to know each other better so we can join each other's Linked-In networks."

3. **Delete**. The invitation will be moved to the trash.

4. **Archive**. The invitation will be stored in your archive file, which gives you the ability to reconsider accepting the invitation at a later time. I use the archive function quite often, but there is one thing I do before I archive someone's invitation: I look at his profile and see whether he is somebody I should at least consider having a meeting with. Remember, this person found you, so he is probably interested in building a business relationship with you. Look at his profile to see if there is something interesting there before you put his invitation in your archive file, where you may forget about it entirely.

Figure 12.8: Consider all of your options when responding to an invitation.

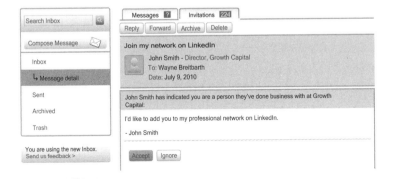

5. **Ignore**. The invitation will be put into the archive file and marked "Ignore." Before deciding to ignore an invitation, follow the same procedure that I suggested for archiving invitations: Check out the person's profile to determine whether there might be a reason to meet him or her. After selecting "Ignore," you will have two additional options— "I don't know them" or "Report as spam." This allows you to report to LinkedIn that this individual might not be using LinkedIn appropriately.

6. **Forward**. If you wish to make an inquiry concerning this person before you decide whether to accept his or her invitation, you can forward the invitation to any of your first-level connections who might possess useful information.

Connecting with Competitors

One question that comes up quite frequently is, "Would you let competitors be connected to you at the first level?" My immediate response is "No!" It does not make good business sense to allow your competitors to have a list of the people who are most important to you. You are basically handing them your Outlook database. There are, however, certain industries in which your competitors may also be your suppliers or vendors, and you will need to weigh the risk and reward of allowing those individuals to be part of your network.

One of the few times I used the "I don't know them" option was when one of my direct competitors, whom I had never met, attempted to connect with me on LinkedIn. There was no way I was going to give her access to the network I have worked so hard to develop over the course of my lifetime. So I promptly told LinkedIn I don't know her. Something tells me she was not surprised by my response.

Monitoring Your Growing Network

Once you've started to build your LinkedIn network, you can easily keep track of the number of new people added to your network since a certain date. Select "Contacts" on the top toolbar and then "Network Statistics" to view information about your total number of connections (see Figure 12.9). You will be amazed at how quickly you continue to add people to your network, not only at the first level but also at the second and third levels. You will find a summary of this information on the right side of your home page. I typically pick up about 8,500 people per day. Although I am not aware of the names of these people or who in my network has connected with them, I do know I am 8,500 people closer to finding that million-cubicle job than I was yesterday. Even when I am at the beach or hiking in the Rocky Mountains, I am adding about 8,500 people per day to my network. Now doesn't that bring new meaning to the word *vacation*! And there is no question in my mind that one day these connections will pay off in a big way.

Figure 12.9: You will be amazed by how quickly your network grows.

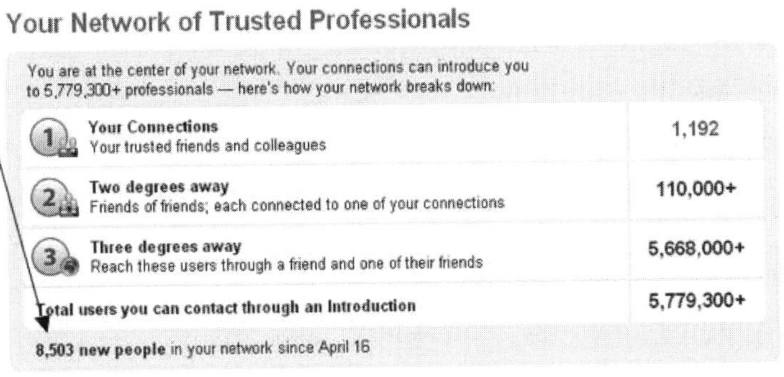

Your Network of Trusted Professionals

You are at the center of your network. Your connections can introduce you to 5,779,300+ professionals — here's how your network breaks down:

Your Connections Your trusted friends and colleagues	1,192
Two degrees away Friends of friends; each connected to one of your connections	110,000+
Three degrees away Reach these users through a friend and one of their friends	5,668,000+
Total users you can contact through an Introduction	5,779,300+

8,503 new people in your network since April 16

Tags

Once you've got all these connections, you'll want to use tags to sort them for easy reference. LinkedIn defines tags as "simple keywords that you can create to organize your connections for quick filtering on LinkedIn." To use this feature, go to "Contacts" on the top toolbar, then click "My Connections," and then click "Tags." Once you have tagged all of your connections that fall into a particular category, LinkedIn will create a list of those connections. Examples of tags that I have found useful include "bankers," "insurance agents," and "customers." As you spend time using this feature, you will find more ways to use tags to help you organize your network, which can save you time when you need to locate or contact a particular person or group within your network.

"Who's Viewed My Profile?"

LinkedIn also allows users to see how many people are looking at their profile with the "Who's Viewed My Profile?" feature, which you'll find in the column on the right side of the LinkedIn home page (see Figure 12.10). This is an interesting box to click on from time to time, but don't expect to see the name of the person who looked at your profile. You may instead see any of the following information about the person: job title, type of company or industry, company name, or location. From this information, you can sometimes guess who viewed your profile and perhaps may be interested in meeting you.

The "Who's Viewed My Profile?" section can also help you identify whether you are increasing your activity and presence on LinkedIn; it will display information like "Your profile has been viewed by 22 people in the last 3 days. Yesterday, you appeared in search results 7 times." As with all networking, increasing your activity has the potential to increase relationships, which may lead to increased business.

Figure 12.10: More looks at your profile should create more business opportunities.

Who's Viewed My Profile?	
21	Your profile has been viewed by 21 people in the past 3 days.
29	You have shown up in search results 29 times in the past 3 days.

Taking advantage of the features explained in this chapter will enable you to quickly add a large number of connections. You'll be on your way to building that big muskie net, so that when you search for new contacts, you will have plenty of people to choose from.

APPLYING THE POWER FORMULA

- Making connections using the steps outlined in this chapter may take you six to eight hours to complete, but it's well worth the effort. Every one of your **unique relationships** gives you lots of Number 2's and 3's, and any of them could be the person you want to meet.

- These steps work more effectively when you have thoroughly outlined your **unique experience** in the Experience and Education sections. If you fail to list a job or an educational experience, you will miss out on potential credibility as well as the opportunity to make valuable connections with people you met while gaining that **unique experience**.

CHAPTER 13

Keywords Are King

Maximizing Your Ability to Find and Be Found by Others

By this time you are probably tired of me talking about the importance of keywords. However, when I teach my classes, I find that many people are not well versed on the logic and rules of keywords and searching.

You have invested a lot of time and effort in creating a perfect profile and building your list of connections, so that when you pull out that muskie net, you can expect to catch lots of potential connections. Understanding the rules presented in this chapter will help you maximize your effectiveness on LinkedIn by giving you much stronger search results.

Searching on LinkedIn works in much the same way as searching elsewhere on the Internet; it is based on Boolean logic. Here are a few of the basic rules of Boolean logic and examples of how you can use them effectively.

Exact Phrases

If you are looking for a specific group of words in a certain order, put that group of words in quotation marks. For example, the search term **interior design** should be put in quotes; otherwise you will get results that include pages where **interior** and **design** show up separately rather than pages where the phrase **interior design** appears.

The "And" Function

Placing the upper-case word **AND** or the plus sign (+) between search terms shows you search results that contain all of the words or phrases you entered. For example, if I am looking for someone who has both **office furniture** and **interior design** in her profile, I would type in either **"office furniture" AND "interior design"** or **"office furniture" + "interior design."** However, you can leave the "AND" or plus sign out, and LinkedIn will assume that there is an "AND" between the two terms (in other words, **"office furniture" "interior design"** would yield the same result as the other searches).

The "Or" Function

Placing an upper-case **OR** between search terms shows you results that contain any one of the search terms but not necessarily both. A search for **CPA OR owner** would give you results for all people who have either the word **CPA** or **owner** somewhere in their profile.

The "Not" Function

Placing the minus sign (-) or the word **NOT** in all caps before a search term excludes that term from the results. For example, if you were looking for someone who is in sales but not in marketing, you would type in **sales NOT marketing** or **sales - marketing**, which will show you profiles that contain the word **sales** but not the word **marketing**.

There are many articles on the Internet that discuss further principles of Boolean logic; you can find them through a quick search. Most of us who spend time developing our LinkedIn networks expect a return on our investment, and becoming proficient at keyword searching is one of the most important steps toward realizing that goal.

Keyword Optimizing Your Profile

Now let's discuss your own keywords and the steps that will help ensure you're on the top of the list when people search LinkedIn for keywords related to what you do. Improving your ranking is very similar to the work search engine optimization companies do in order to move business websites up in the search results on Google. If you are a business owner with a website, you probably paid lots of money to have your website optimized for keyword searching. Your LinkedIn profile is your personal website, and this is your chance to keyword optimize your profile—without having to pay tons of money to an SEO expert. Follow these steps:

1. Go to the Advanced People Search function of LinkedIn and put your most important keywords in the Keyword box (see Figure 13.1). For me it's the phrase "office furniture." If you serve a certain region of the country, select the radius and zip code that best covers your market (see Figure 13.2). Once you hit the blue Search button at the bottom of the page, scroll through the search results and

note exactly where your profile shows up. If it's not on the first page, you have some work to do—but even if it does show up on the first page, your goal should be to become the first search result in your region for that keyword or set of keywords.

Figure 13.1: Start the process of keyword optimizing your profile.

Figure 13.2: Carefully defining your market will result in more meaningful search results.

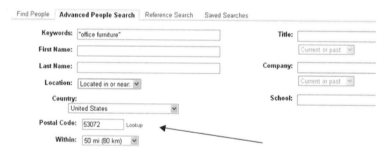

2. Revise your profile, adding the top keywords you identified in step 1 to any and all of the following five areas: Headline, Summary, Specialties, Position Title, and Position

Description. Based on the blogs I have read, you get extra LinkedIn search weighting by having these words in your headline and in your position titles, and my research backs up that claim. Also try to get these keywords dropped into any new recommendations you receive. In my situation, I might be tempted to simply list "office furniture, office furniture, office furniture" wherever I can, but remember that you want your profile to be understandable and readable. Do your best to incorporate the keywords naturally. Once you have added additional keywords to your profile, perform the same search and see if you have moved up in the results.

I pride myself on being the number-one hit when I search for office furniture in the Milwaukee area. There have been times when I lost that position and had to work very hard to move myself back to the top. Be diligent in continuing to add keywords that will improve your search ranking—you want to be at the top of the list, where people will notice you.

3. Perform a search for additional keywords that relate to your company and/or industry. Have fun experimenting with different keywords, combinations of keywords, and complex searches. Be sure to save the most relevant complex searches (as discussed in Chapter 10). Remember, one of these searches just might be the one that helps you find the person who will lead you to that million-cubicle deal.

APPLYING THE POWER FORMULA

- Keywords are king. Combinations of keywords are the king and his court. Be sure to look at your competitors' profiles in detail and scout out what words they use to explain their **unique experience**. You may find some you have missed.

- You may want to survey some of your best customers and ask them, "If you were to search for me or my company on the Internet, what words would you use?" Use these **unique relationships** and your ability to ask them these types of questions to your advantage.

CHAPTER 14

How Do Companies Fit into the LinkedIn Landscape?

Researching Companies on LinkedIn and
Other Company-Related Matters

One very useful function of LinkedIn is the ability to learn more about companies. Rumor has it that the company section may become one of the exclusive benefits of paid LinkedIn accounts, but at the present time it is still free—and very powerful.

When you click the "More" tab on the toolbar at the top of any LinkedIn page and then select "Companies," you can then search for companies using either keywords or a company name. When you click on a company in the search results, you will get what LinkedIn refers to as a company profile. I do not like the use of the word *profile* in reference to company pages because it implies that companies have the same networking capabilities as individuals on LinkedIn, which is not the case. However, there is plenty of useful information contained on company profiles, and the LinkedIn company database is growing rapidly. In fact, many people consider it more useful than Hoover's, which a lot of us access on a fee basis.

On the top left of a company's profile, you will see general company information and the company's logo. When you click "More" below the summary, you will see the Specialties section of the company profile. As we discussed with regard to the Specialties section of an individual's profile, placement of relevant keywords in this section will greatly enhance a company's ability to be found in LinkedIn user searches. On the lower right-hand side of this screen, you will find company statistics, which are either entered by a designated company official or garnered by LinkedIn from public information.

The list below is certainly not an exhaustive catalog of the information available on a company's LinkedIn page, but these are some of the items I have found useful—particularly when searching for potential customers and new employees as well as attempting to stay on top of what my competitors are doing. Many of them are accessed by clicking "Check out insightful statistics about [company name] employees," located in the right column of the company profile.

- A list of all company employees who are in your network
- The total number of employees who have LinkedIn accounts
- Names of new hires at the company
- A list of the company's current job postings on LinkedIn, accessed by clicking the "Careers" tab at the top of the company's profile
- New titles of company employees who have updated their LinkedIn accounts to reflect a recent promotion
- Names of people who have recently departed from the company

- A list of the geographical areas that employees of the company call home
- A list of the employees who have the most recommendations
- A list of the other company profiles people are viewing
- Information on where employees worked before and after their employment with the company

On a company's profile page you can also find graphs that include statistics LinkedIn has generated about the company's employees, including:

- Job function composition (e.g., percentage of employees doing general and administrative work, research and development)
- Years of work experience
- Highest educational degree attained
- Most common universities attended

My teenager might say, "Too much information!" Granted—you may not find all this information useful. However, once you realize what type of information is available about the company as a whole and about its past and present employees and how you may be connected to them, you can begin to put together a strategy for using this information to accomplish your goals.

When you have identified a company or organization in which you have an ongoing interest, LinkedIn gives you the opportunity to receive notification of any changes to that company's profile page. This can be done by clicking the words "Follow [company name]" located next to the star on the right side of the page. You will then receive notification of any changes to the page as part of your network updates. This form of "stalking" is an effective way to keep track of your targets, which could include current and prospective customers, competitors, or organizations with which you are seeking employment.

You have already discovered the many benefits of searching for people on LinkedIn, and searching for companies can be equally beneficial. There are numerous criteria you can use to find businesses. Let's say you want to find an office furniture dealership in your area but also want to be sure the dealership can provide interior design services. You would enter "office furniture" and "interior design" in the Company Name or Keyword box. To regionalize the search, select "Located in or near" from the Location pull-down menu. Additional options for country and postal code will then become available. You can modify your results by industry and limit your search to companies of a certain size, companies with employees who are first- or second-degree connections, or companies that have jobs posted on LinkedIn.

If you are the person responsible for setting up your company profile on LinkedIn, you can get started by going to the Companies home page and clicking on "Add a Company" at the top right of the page. You can then enter whatever basic organizational information your company wants to share with the LinkedIn community and the entire Google world. Your company's LinkedIn profile will show up when someone searches for your company using Google, and many times it will be near the top of the list. Be sure to carefully draft your company's LinkedIn profile so that its story is presented in a very positive and professional manner.

Social Media Policies and Procedures

Social media is creating many great business development opportunities, not only for individuals but for companies as well. If you are a company leader or the person responsible for organizational policies and procedures, you will need to decide whether your company will embrace these new social media tools and—if so— how you will develop a set of effective company policies relating to them. No one wants more policies, but what can be a great tool can also be a great detriment to the business if used improperly. In the classes I lead, questions about companies and social media come up more and more, and it is very important that you think about the following items as you draft your company's official position on LinkedIn:

1. What rules do you want to have about LinkedIn usage on company time?
2. What branding message do you want shared with the public—not only on the company profile page but also on each individual profile page that mentions your company?
3. What keywords and descriptions of your company do you want included in your employees' profiles?
4. Will you allow employees to receive recommendations from and write recommendations for your clients or customers?
5. Will you allow employees to write recommendations for each other?

Considering these questions may make you doubt that you should even play the social media game. But do not be discouraged. More and more companies are gaining market share by effectively using social media to communicate with customers, employees, and business partners, and you do not want to be left behind. It's just a matter of taking the lead and having enough knowledge to feel comfortable with your company's presence in this sphere.

Get started by bringing together a group of people to discuss how you can consistently brand your company using tools like LinkedIn, Facebook, Twitter, and others. Discuss your strategy for communicating via social media because your company's message can become inconsistent when each individual employee uses his or her own style to present information about the organization. Although LinkedIn and other social media sites are designed to be about individuals rather than companies, your efforts to strategize with a committee of your employees and colleagues will help your company have a stronger and more consistent online presence.

You will find that individuals from the Facebook generation will be very excited to give input. They tend to love social networking tools, to the point that many do not even regard it as work. In contrast, many of us from non-Facebook generations find social networking frustrating and time-consuming, and we may not understand the results that our efforts can produce. The committee you put together should consist of people who are willing to lead the charge and who actually enjoy being involved in high-level strategy sessions about branding and marketing for the company.

APPLYING THE POWER FORMULA

- Nothing benefits your company's search rankings more than you and all your employees having lots of first-degree connections. This is yet another way those **unique relationships** pay off.

- Be certain that you use the Specialties section of your company profile for some of the same keywords you used in the Specialties section of your personal profile.

- Do not underestimate the power of telling your company's **unique** story in the Overview section of the company profile. This may be the only bit of information a person sees before contacting you. Think of it as a free listing in a 100-million-person searchable database. Now that's power.

CHAPTER 15

Revving Up Your LinkedIn Efforts by Joining Groups

The Power of LinkedIn Groups

Social networking is all about people coming together, sharing information, and forming communities, and LinkedIn is no exception. The Groups function on LinkedIn is one of the most effective tools on the site for interacting with people in your industry, region, or specialty. My research shows that LinkedIn users rate groups as the second most important part of LinkedIn. (People-searching is rated the most useful function.)

Groups are very easy to join, and you can belong to as many as fifty at any time. I recommend joining close to that amount. Here are some of the most compelling reasons to join groups:

1. You will be found.
2. You will find others who have similar affiliations or interests.

3. Joining groups in which your customers, suppliers, or vendors hang out is a way to connect, answer questions, and share resources, expertise, and events.

4. You will find job opportunities, because every group has a tab for available positions at members' companies.

5. You can become a credible expert by answering questions and posting articles of interest for the entire group to see.

6. In groups, people talk about events they are involved in, and this may help you find activities of interest to you.

7. You can promote an event you are hosting to a group of people who have the same interests.

8. You can search within groups and communicate with members to whom you are not officially connected.

Let me give you an example of this last benefit because it is not always appreciated or understood. If you look at the group Link Up Milwaukee (see Figure 15.1), you will see that, with 7,745 members, it is the largest group in the region. The larger the group, the larger the pool of LinkedIn members available for you to search for high-value contacts. Searching groups is a very powerful tool in building your muskie net; being a member of Link Up Milwaukee allows me to keyword search those 7,745

Figure 15.1: Take advantage of the searching power large groups can provide.

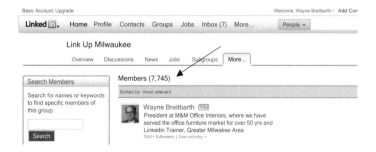

members for people I want to meet—whether directly or through a mutual connection. And because I am a member of Link Up Milwaukee, I can send direct messages to all my fellow group members, although I cannot look at their connections and don't have the other privileges of a Number 1 connection.

Groups like this one present yet another opportunity for connection with people beyond the traditional phone call, e-mail, or snail mail. However, even though I think groups are very valuable, I am not a fan of asking people to join your network simply because you belong to the same LinkedIn group. You will get invitations like that, but remember—you want to connect with people you know and trust.

As I mentioned earlier, you should try to join fifty groups. The reason I suggest joining this many is because different types of groups have different purposes. Groups like Link Up Milwaukee get some mass into your groups, allowing you to be more effective when searching. Then you have groups in your specific industry. You will want to join national, regional, and local groups that focus on your particular specialty. For example, if you are an accountant, you may want to join CPA, which is a national group with more than 7,000 members. This will allow you to find information about national events, educational opportunities, and industry trends. If your accounting practice is in Wisconsin, you could join WICPA (Wisconsin Institute of CPAs), which has more than 1,000 members and would give you access to regional information, such as proposed statewide legislation related to accounting issues.

Locally, you could join the Milwaukee & Waukesha Area Accounting Professionals group, which includes more than 50 accounting professionals who share ideas and job leads. If your firm specializes in accounting for nonprofits, joining NonProfit

MidWest (350+ members) would give you an opportunity to identify potential clients who do business in your geographic region. The fifty groups you join will depend on your strategy, what your products or services are, and where you provide those products or services.

The types of groups you should join are:

- "Birds of a feather" groups—alumni associations, chambers, clubs, religious organizations, hobby groups, etc.
- Industry groups (both inside and outside of your region)
- LinkedIn or other social media user groups (These groups concentrate on helping each other be more productive on these sites.)
- Regional super groups (like Link Up Milwaukee)

Once you join a large number of communities, you may want to turn off the e-mail notifications for discussions taking place in some of the larger groups—the ones you may have joined solely because of the size of their memberships. Many times the topics being discussed in these large groups will not be of interest to you. For instance, in Wisconsin, a popular group to join is the Green Bay Packers Fans group. With over 2,300 members, it gives you lots of searching power. However, you would undoubtedly want to turn off the e-mail notifications, unless you are interested in the constant Brett Favre banter. You can turn off e-mail notifications by changing the settings in the individual group's Settings section (see Figure 15.2). However, be sure to leave e-mail notifications on for the groups whose discussions you are interested in monitoring.

Checking out the groups to which your connections belong is the best way to start finding groups. You can also search the

Groups Directory using keywords. To do this, select "Groups Directory" from the "Groups" pull-down menu in the top tool-bar; the search box is on the upper left.

As with many other aspects of LinkedIn, successfully using the Groups function comes down to deciding what you want to accomplish on LinkedIn and finding ways to achieve it strategically. Joining these communities is just another way to expand your capabilities and reach on LinkedIn.

Figure 15.2: You control whether you receive e-mail notifications.

APPLYING THE POWER FORMULA

- If you have worked hard at traditional networking, you have undoubtedly been involved with numerous networking groups. These groups have hopefully afforded you a significant number of **unique relationships**, which now will become Number 1 connections on LinkedIn. These same groups may have LinkedIn counterparts that can jumpstart your search for useful connections and increase the power of your searches.

CHAPTER 16

Show Me the Money!

What Are the Power Users
Doing on LinkedIn?

I consider power users to be those people who are obtaining significant results in response to their efforts on LinkedIn. The common thread among these successful users is a well-developed strategy and consistent execution of that strategy. Creative and efficient use of the many available features on LinkedIn enables these users to maximize their time spent on LinkedIn and achieve (and in many cases exceed) their specific goals.

I have many opportunities to poll LinkedIn users about the tangible benefits they are receiving from their use of LinkedIn. Though most users can readily report the number of connections they have made through LinkedIn, some are at a loss to identify specific results they have achieved. Inquiry as to their LinkedIn strategy typically results in a response like, "Well, I'm adding lots of connections!" Adding connections without a clear plan can be just as unproductive as physical networking without a strategy for how to meet the right people. Before you spend one more moment on building your network or improving your profile, sit down and document exactly what you are trying to accomplish by using LinkedIn.

Here are some questions to ask yourself as you develop your LinkedIn strategy:

- Can LinkedIn help me find a job?
- Would it be helpful to build a network of people in related industries?
- Can I leverage my relationships with current customers to work toward gaining additional customers?
- Do I want to expand my network of suppliers and gain access to products or services that complement what I sell or provide?
- Can I find new groups or associations that might provide me with speaking opportunities?
- Do I need to hire employees with specific expertise and experiences?
- Could LinkedIn help me become recognized as one of the experts in my industry?
- Can I increase my brand and overall credibility in the marketplace?

This list is not meant to be exhaustive, but it may assist you in identifying potential strategies for achieving measurable results with LinkedIn. I do not believe you should spend time on LinkedIn or any other social media site until you have outlined what you hope to accomplish. Once you have identified your goals, you can identify the strategy that will best help you reach those goals.

The semiannual poll I give, in addition to the countless personal conversations I have with users, enable me to discover how people are using LinkedIn to obtain results. I have used that information to put together a list of the top ten steps you can take to expand your business, add value to your relationships, and improve your overall effectiveness on LinkedIn.

Here they are, David Letterman style, in increasing order of importance. Paul, music please . . .

10. Consider investing in a $200 Flip cam and posting videos of individuals at your organization "doing what they do"—including designers, service people, and other employees. Ask them questions about the company and the quality of their work while they are in action and post the videos in the SlideShare or Google Presentation applications on your LinkedIn profile. You can also use the Flip cam to record customer testimonials about what differentiates you and your company.

9. Before you head out of town for a business meeting, do a keyword search in the area of the country you will be visiting to see if any of your Number 1 connections have contacts there—you may be able to get together with one or more of them to share ideas. As discussed in Chapter 9, you can use the Events application to check out events being held in the region where you will be traveling.

8. Create your own LinkedIn group for members of your industry (or members of a segment of your industry) who live in your region. Set it up as a closed group, one in which you get to control who can join. Once you have established the group, be sure to add value on a consistent basis by sharing helpful articles and links. Consider

hosting one or two events each year where members can meet up in person. If possible, make these exclusive events with well-known industry speakers. Establishing yourself as a thought leader in your market should be one of your primary goals on LinkedIn, and leading a vibrant group is a strong step toward that objective.

7. Write a recommendation for an acquaintance with whom you would like to develop a broader and deeper relationship.

6. Constantly be on the lookout for articles and websites that show expertise in your industry, and consistently post them as status updates, SlideShow videos, or Box.net files. When you do this, LinkedIn will alert all of your first-degree connections about the new item you have posted on your profile. If the item is particularly significant, you may want to add a statement in your Summary section that directs people to the section in your profile where the file resides. For example, one of my Box.net files is a PDF file titled "What Makes a Great Workplace?" In my Summary section, I could reference this white paper by saying, "See my Box.net files below for an informative article about what makes a great workplace." This not only tells the reader that I am an expert but also that I want to help him.

5. Set a goal to get an introduction—through LinkedIn or the good old-fashioned way—from one of your Number 1 connections every week. The introduction requests (hopefully for Number 2 connections) should be the result of strategic advanced searches for your typical client or customer.

4. Create a saved search using the keywords that are most important to you so that LinkedIn will notify you when someone who meets those search criteria enters your extended network. For example, because architects design buildings that will eventually require office furniture, I am always interested in forging new relationships with members of the architectural community. Therefore, a saved search with the keywords *architect* and *architectural* that targets my geographic market will likely lead to future business opportunities.

3. On a weekly basis, review the first-level connections of your own strategically important first-level connections. My life and disability insurance agent, who happens to be a fraternity brother, has consistently done a great job of asking for referrals when we meet for our semi-annual breakfast or lunch. Now that I am using LinkedIn, we spend that time talking about our kids and hobbies or reminiscing about the good old days; he can look at my Number 1 connections anytime he chooses. Some people choose to turn off the ability for others to view their Number 1 connections, so you may not be able to do this with everyone in your network. However, the default setting on LinkedIn makes your first-degree connections visible to your network.

2. Print the profile of anyone you are meeting for the first time, even if you are just meeting him or her over the phone. This will help you understand that person's business and expertise, and it will enable you to identify common interests and conversation-starters for your initial contact. Most businesspeople are always looking for ways

to connect with people on a personal level before jumping into a business discussion. That business professional has put all this information in her profile because she is proud of her interests and accomplishments and wants you to know and ask about them. This is a great way to show that you do your homework and care about her as a person—not just as a potential sale.

1. Update your status several times each week using the box near the top of your home page that says "Share an update." Much like Twitter, this feature allows you to post short updates to your LinkedIn network. Since the status update does not go out as a message, you do not need to be concerned about annoying people; the content you type in this box will only appear in the Network Activity column of each of your connections' home screens. Some people choose to receive a weekly e-mail that shows their network's activity, and those people can also view your update there. Status updates are one of the most powerful functions of LinkedIn. Use them to share the following items with your network:

- Events you will be attending
- Helpful websites and articles you have found
- Short tips or suggestions that showcase your expertise
- Unique stories and ideas from people you have recently met
- Questions about which you would like to poll your network
- Inquiries about the types of job opportunities you are looking for

Spend some time looking at the status updates of the people in your network to get a feel for what is typically shared here. I use the status box in a number of ways. On a recent Friday afternoon, my service manager informed me that he needed four men for a weeklong project that was beginning in ten days. Since my network is loaded with fifty-year-old people who are always interested in ensuring their college-age sons are gainfully employed, I posted this need in my status update. Forty-five minutes later, I had five strong young men whose parents convinced them they should help me out and pick up some quick cash to pay for a few of their own expenses.

I have used the status box to help my daughter secure a summer job and to assist a nonprofit group in locating tents for an event they were hosting. It would probably have taken several hundred phone calls to get the results I got from simply typing my request into the status box and clicking "Send." However, because LinkedIn is a business site, I would recommend that you use this tool sparingly for personal requests. Even though many people in your network will be more than willing to help you out both personally and professionally, it's best to not overload their Network Activity columns with requests.

You now know the ten actions that LinkedIn power users find most useful and effective. Whether you choose to incorporate all ten of them into your LinkedIn strategy or simply focus on the ones that most closely fit your personal networking goals, you will certainly be working toward expanding your business, adding value to your relationships, and improving your overall effectiveness on LinkedIn.

CHAPTER 17

Your Account, Your Settings— Your Way

Setting Your Preferences and Using the LinkedIn Help Centers

You will find that LinkedIn gives you an extensive amount of user control and many resources for solving problems and learning even more about LinkedIn's features.

To access many useful account controls, click "Settings," which you will find under your name on the top right of any screen. The Settings page is the control panel for everything you have the ability to set, turn off/on, and expand on your LinkedIn account. There are numerous settings you may want to explore— many of which are self-explanatory—but I am going to address the ones you will need to understand up front as well as the ones that people ask me about most frequently:

- **Public Profile.** Found under "Profile Settings," this is where you can control which, if any, of the items in your profile will be displayed to those people who are not on LinkedIn but find your public LinkedIn profile as a result of searching your name on the Internet.

- **Receiving Messages**. This setting, found under the "Email Notifications" heading, allows you to control which types of e-mails you receive from LinkedIn and how often you get them. These e-mails include summaries of your network activity and discussions in groups you belong to. For the most part, your choices are immediately, weekly, or never.

- **Groups Order and Display**. This setting (under "Groups") controls how group logos are displayed on your profile and also enables you to choose the order in which your groups appear. Placing certain groups near the top of the list may increase the credibility of your profile and advance your personal brand. If you are concerned that your membership in a particular group or association might alienate a segment of your customer base or potential customer base, you can turn off the display of that group. I have seen this used most often with regard to political and religious group affiliations.

- **E-mail Addresses**. Be sure to associate all the e-mail addresses you have or have had in the past with your Linked-In account. You can easily do this by clicking on this setting (found under the "Personal Information" heading). You may want your primary address (the one to which all of your LinkedIn e-mails come) to be a nonwork address. I have heard horror stories from people who lost their jobs and had a very difficult time getting access to their LinkedIn account.

- **Profile Views**. This setting is found in the "Privacy Settings" section. If you want to have your name and headline show up in "Who's Viewed My Profile?" instead of simply your title and general industry information, change the setting here to "My name and headline." I recommend this change from the default because it is another opportunity to get your brand in front of LinkedIn members. Think about what we all pay "per touch" in conventional advertising. Here is a freebie!

- **Profile and Status Updates**. You can modify the way others are notified using this setting, found under "Privacy Settings." The default is that LinkedIn notifies your network every time you make a change to your profile or write a recommendation for one of your connections. I love this, because your name and the fact you made those changes shows up on the home page of every one of your first-level connections. However, if you are spending the weekend working on many changes to your profile, you will want to turn this off. Then, after you make the final changes, turn it back on and—presto—LinkedIn tells your network something has changed, and hopefully your connections will take a look at it.

My advice is to click on each of the settings and find out what options are available to you. The settings I have outlined above are the ones I am asked about most often, but you may find others that will be useful for your situation. There are other ways to change some of these settings, but it is easiest to access them from the Settings page because they are laid out in dashboard fashion.

Paid vs. Free Accounts

People also constantly ask me whether I use a free or paid account. To view a chart that outlines the additional features you will receive with the various types of paid accounts, click "Settings," which you will find under your name on the top right of any screen, and then click "Compare account types" (see Figure 17.1). Consider moving to one of the paid accounts if you are:

1. A human resources professional
2. A recruiter
3. Someone who consistently runs into the screen that says you should upgrade

Figure 17.1: A free account may be all you need.

If you are regularly seeing the screen that suggests you should upgrade, you are probably using a LinkedIn feature that is working for you, and you may want to consider going to one of the paid accounts. For example, if you tend to run out of InMails, introductions, or saved searches, you may want to consider upgrading your LinkedIn account. In general, I do not recommend moving to a paid account unless you fall into one of the three categories listed above. However, in order to encourage more of us to pay for LinkedIn on a monthly basis, there will undoubtedly be more and more valuable new features available exclusively to paid subscribers. Setting up folders for profiles is a feature that is of interest to me, and I have considered moving to a paid account in order to access it.

LinkedIn Learning Center and Customer Service Center

Whether you have a free or paid account, LinkedIn has a significant amount of instructional materials available within the site. You can access them by selecting "More" on the toolbar at the top of the screen and then choosing "Learning Center." Here you will find a large list of tutorials, including videos, tips, and user guides. The Learning Center will be particularly important to you when you are starting out on LinkedIn, but LinkedIn provides extensive information and advice for advanced users as well, and they do a good job of updating these resources frequently.

LinkedIn also has a Customer Service Center, which you may find to be quite useful. Click "Customer Service" on the bottom toolbar, and you will then be able to search for the information you desire. If you do not find an answer to your question, you can contact LinkedIn by clicking "Contact Us" on the Customer Service Center toolbar. In my experience, Customer Service usually responds within a couple days, which is quite remarkable considering I do not have a paid account. And each time I have asked a question, the answer has solved my problem.

Take full advantage of the extensive user controls and helpful resources LinkedIn provides. Adjust the settings to reflect your personal preferences, and you will gain the level of comfort and privacy you desire.

CHAPTER 18

A Job Seeker's New Best Friend
LinkedIn—The World's Largest Internet-Based Resume Database

This chapter is for those of you who are in the process of looking for employment, whether you are seeking to reenter the job market or looking to change or upgrade your current situation. While some of these tips and strategies will overlap with previous chapters, it's important for you to understand the arsenal of tools LinkedIn offers job seekers.

As a job seeker, LinkedIn will be your new best friend because it offers the following valuable capabilities:

- Yours can be one of 100 million "resumes on steroids" employers can search to locate a candidate they would love to hire.
- You can give a vast amount of detail about your skills and experience on your profile, as discussed in Chapter 5.

- You can search for recruiters in any region of the country who specialize in placing people with your expertise.
- You can find out which of your first-, second-, or third-level connections know people at the organization you are targeting.

As I teach LinkedIn training classes, I find that both recruiters and human resources professionals use LinkedIn extensively, many finding themselves checking their account multiple times a day. As a job seeker, that means you should spend a significant amount of your time each day on LinkedIn, networking and optimizing your information to stand out to the people you want to be found by.

Use the following checklist to help ensure you are availing yourself of the myriad features of LinkedIn that can assist you in finding and securing that next great position:

☐ Be sure your headline states that you are looking for a job. Use very specific language, such as "actively pursuing a job as an IT professional in the fluid power industry" or something of that nature. Your friends want to help you, and your headline should scream out the fact that you are seeking employment and need their help. (If you are brave, you could even try a headline like "President of In-Between Opportunities.")

☐ Do not list your last job as your current job or people may become confused as to whether you are looking for a job or not. LinkedIn requires you to put a current company name in, which makes this a little tricky; some people put "Currently seeking employment at no name company" in the Current Job field. Play around with it and see what you like best. If you are consulting while you seek full-time employment (or if you just list your current job as "Consultant" in an attempt to "look employed"), you may want to say something like "Part-time consultant seeking full-time employment."

☐ The first paragraph of your Summary and Specialties sections should explain in a couple of sentences what you consider to be the perfect position for you, and the rest of the detail in your profile should support that. Be certain this paragraph explains to the reader in clear language your goals and your ideal job, so that if he has that job open at his company, he will be able to say, "I just found the person I'm looking for."

☐ Make sure you have two or three recommendations for each job. These recommendations should be specific; they need to differentiate you from the job-seeking masses. As you wait in line for an interview, your profile may be sitting on a human resources professional's desk alongside the profile of the person interviewing directly after you. If you have no recommendations and she has twenty—two or three for each job, in addition to recommendations for her educational entries—who do you think the interviewer will pick? Put yourself in the offensive position, and do not let this happen to you. Go out and get those recommendations. They will serve you well.

☐ Be sure to load your Specialties section with the keywords recruiters will be looking for—terms relating to specific software, processes, degrees, specialties, and training, as well as any other words and phrases that speak to your credibility and education.

☐ Using Box.net files, SlideShare, or Google Presentation, post items such as your resume, your portfolio, and articles you have written. Consider including a slide show that outlines your career, and you may also want to post a video resume to YouTube and link to it through the Websites, SlideShare, or Google Presentation sections on your profile. Video resumes are a very effective tool, and making one is as simple as picking up a $200 Flip cam (or borrowing one from a gadget-loving friend) and plugging it into your computer. A video resume shows your personality, your story, your passion—and the fact that you are technologically savvy.

☐ In your Contact Settings, which you can edit by going to the very bottom of your profile, be certain to check the box next to "Career opportunities" (see Figure 18.1), as long as you are not concerned about your current employer knowing you are looking for a job. Many HR professionals and recruiters filter out candidates who do not have this box checked in order to be sure they are looking at people who are actually seeking employment.

Figure 18.1: Let the world know you are looking for a job.

Opportunity Preferences

What kinds of opportunities would you like to receive?

☐ Career opportunities
☐ Consulting offers
☐ New ventures
☑ Job inquiries

☑ Expertise requests
☑ Business deals
☑ Personal reference requests
☑ Requests to reconnect

What advice would you give to users considering contacting you?

> If you are interested in the great professionals from M&M Office Interiors giving you "The Space You Want and The Experience You Deserve" contact me right away. I

Include comments on your availability, types of projects or opportunities that interest you, and what information you'd like to see included in a request. To avoid unwanted contacts, **do not** include contact information, since your response will be visible to your entire network. See examples.

☐ Complete your profile 100 percent, and you will be forty times more effective.

☐ Use LinkedIn Jobs to search for opportunities. You can access this feature by clicking on "Jobs" in the top toolbar. In this section, you can search for jobs that are posted directly on LinkedIn. In the Advanced Search in the Jobs tab, you can narrow your search using not only keywords (see Figure 18.2) but job functions, experience levels, and other criteria (see Figure 18.3). You can save ten job searches.

Figure 18.2: Take advantage of LinkedIn's immense database of job opportunities.

Figure 18.3: Get specific and uncover the perfect job.

Functions:	✓ All Job Functions
	☐ Accounting/Auditing
	☐ Administrative
	☐ Advertising
	☐ Analyst

Industries:	✓ All Industries
	☐ Accounting
	☐ Airlines/Aviation
	☐ Alternative Dispute Resolution
	☐ Alternative Medicine

Experience:	✓ Any Level
	☐ Executive
	☐ Director
	☐ Mid-Senior level
	☐ Associate

When Posted:	✓ Any Time
	☐ 1 day ago
	☐ 2-7 days ago
	☐ 8-14 days ago
	☐ 15-30 days ago

Sort By: Relevance

☐ One of the major benefits of the Jobs feature on Linked-In is that when your search brings up a job you're interested in, you can search for people in your network who work for that company. When a job is posted directly on LinkedIn, you can often see the name of the person who created the listing and find out whether you are connected to him or her (see Figure 18.4).

Figure 18.4: Using a name and title sure beats "To Whom It May Concern."

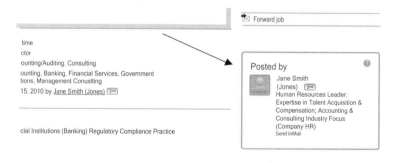

☐ After you have applied for a job in whatever way the application requires (mail, fax, online, etc.), use Advanced People Search to see if you can locate somebody in your network at the first, second, or third level who works for the company or, better yet, is involved in the Human Resources Department or the department you've applied to. Contacting this person may enable you to get your resume to the top of the stack. By effectively leveraging your network, you can greatly increase your chances of getting that job. Remember, your network would love to help you.

☐ You will find it very advantageous to use the Linked-In JobsInsider tool. This comes as part of the Browser Toolbar, which you can download from the Tools section at the bottom of your LinkedIn screen. Once you download the Browser Toolbar, if you follow a link from LinkedIn to an external job listing—whether on Monster, CareerBuilder, or the company's own website—JobsInsider will alert you to any contacts in your network who work at the company and thus may be able to help you secure the position.

☐ You will find it very helpful to look at the LinkedIn profile of the company you are targeting. Look at the employee list to see if there is anyone who might be able to give you the inside scoop on the position you applied for, the hiring process, the company's political climate. Use the "Follow company" option to keep tabs on the organization on an ongoing basis.

☐ Be sure to update your LinkedIn status periodically (two to three times per week) to remind your network that you are still looking for a job. For example, stating in an update that you will be attending a job fair will not only put your name in front of your network but will also remind your contacts that you need their help in finding a job. Your network will undoubtedly lead you to your next job as long as you keep yourself top of mind among your connections. The status box is a great way to do that.

☐ In each group there is a Jobs tab that lists employment opportunities relevant to that community (see Figure 18.5). Jobs can be posted by any member of the group. If, for example, you are looking for a job as a project manager in the construction business, you will want to join groups related to the construction industry and frequently check the Jobs tabs for new postings. Joining fifty groups on LinkedIn will give you access to fifty job boards. Take advantage of this opportunity.

Figure 18.5: Judiciously joining and being active in groups may be your ticket to the perfect job.

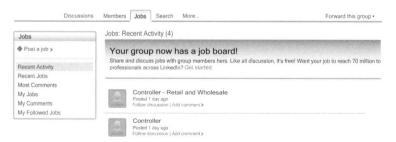

☐ You can also use the Answers section to exhibit your industry expertise. You get to the Answers section by clicking "More" on the top toolbar and then selecting "Answers." The Answers section is a way to get yourself in front of people from industries you have worked in or would like to work in. Spend time answering questions pertaining to industries that are of interest to you. In addition, pose questions you think the network might be interested in getting feedback on.

☐ Use the Events application to find in-person networking opportunities. Remember, part of your day should be spent in face-to-face meetings in which you remind people that you are in the market for a job.

☐ Once you secure an interview, print and review the profile of the person with whom you will be interviewing and look for areas of common interest you can use as discussion starters. You may find it helpful to look over the recommendations the interviewer has written for others; this will tell you what qualities she appreciates in her business associates. Emphasizing the fact that you possess these traits could prove helpful in securing the position.

☐ An experienced recruiter can be very beneficial in finding employment opportunities, and you can find many good recruiters on LinkedIn. An Advanced People Search will help you zero in on the best recruiters for your circumstance.

If you find yourself in job-seeking mode, LinkedIn should be on your computer screen for several hours each day. You will want to follow the suggestions listed here as well as keeping track of who's meeting whom on LinkedIn and strategizing about how you can engage in conversations with people who can help you find your next job.

APPLYING THE POWER FORMULA

- The person who has the most **unique experiences**, along with the most **unique relationships**, will generally find employment more quickly than other job seekers, especially if he has leveraged the full power of LinkedIn.

- When in job-seeking mode, be careful not to rely solely on virtual tools like LinkedIn and forget that you need to create or reestablish **unique relationships** on a face-to-face basis, too.

CHAPTER 19

Ready . . . Set . . . Go!

A Six-Week, Two-Hour-per-Week Road Map to Results

If you are a novice user or have just now decided to take the leap and begin using LinkedIn, I would like to give you a road map for moving forward and executing a LinkedIn strategy. By spending about two hours per week for the next six weeks, you will be able to execute many of the techniques I have presented. You will find and connect with people you know and trust, and the effort you put into creating a beefy profile will increase the likelihood of your being found. Follow this six-week game plan to make sure you cover all your bases and get off to a strong start.

If you are the owner of or a leader within a company, this game plan might also be a valuable tool for you to use. Some of these steps can be delegated to people who have social media expertise and the time to accumulate and draft the information you are going to include in your profile. However, an important point to remember when you are using LinkedIn—or any other social media tool, for that matter—is that you should always personally communicate with your network.

For example, if you are going to delegate a portion of the responsibility for your LinkedIn profile, such as writing portions of the Summary section or adding connections from a card file, be certain that your own personality comes through and that you understand the steps being taken on your behalf. This way, you will avoid having someone come up to you and thank you for connecting on LinkedIn when you have no idea who the person is because one of your assistants added him.

Below I have outlined a six-week road map that will assist you in harnessing the power of LinkedIn. This plan should be extremely valuable if you are just beginning your use of LinkedIn. If your profile is already 100 percent complete and you have a documented LinkedIn strategy, you can use this as a checklist to assure yourself that you are on the right track.

Week 1

- Join LinkedIn.
- Accept any invitations that meet your acceptance criteria.
- Put your most recent jobs into the Experience section of your profile. If you have a current resume, you can import it into LinkedIn to jumpstart the writing process.
- Complete the Education section of your profile.
- Invite five trusted professionals into your network.
- Add a professional-looking photo to your profile.

Week 2

- Accept any invitations that meet your acceptance criteria.
- Invite five more trusted professionals into your network.
- Complete the Experience section of your profile.
- Put your company website on your profile, and give it a description other than the standard "My Company."
- Write a killer 120-word marketing headline that includes important keywords.
- Join five groups. Think industry groups, alumni associations, chambers, and large regional networking groups.

Week 3

- Accept any invitations that meet your acceptance criteria.
- Review the "People You May Know" section and send invitations to anyone you know and trust.
- Request a recommendation from a trusted professional who knows you well enough to write a detailed, keyword-filled testimonial about you.
- Write a recommendation for someone in your network who would really appreciate the props.
- Perform a company search on either a competitor or a target organization.
- Perform an Advanced People Search using the most important keywords for your business or industry in the region you serve. See if you know anyone who comes up in the search results. Send invitations to those who meet your criteria.
- Join five more groups.
- Post a status update that is helpful and/or shows expertise.

Week 4

- Accept any invitations that meet your acceptance criteria.
- Add two more items to your Website section.
- Add any significant volunteer work to your current Experience section.
- Add any specialty classes or technical industry training to your Education section.
- Write a recommendation for someone in your network.
- Be sure your company has all the appropriate information on its LinkedIn company profile.
- Join five more groups.
- Perform a company search on either a competitor or a target organization.
- Perform an Advanced People Search with important keywords, and send invitations to those who meet your criteria.
- Request a recommendation from a professional you know and trust.
- Using a word processing program, create the text for your 2000-character Summary section. Spell-check it and post it on your profile.
- Post a status update that is helpful and/or shows expertise.

Week 5

- Accept any invitations that meet your acceptance criteria.
- Write a recommendation for someone in your network.
- Join five more groups.
- Perform three keyword searches in Advanced People Search and save them.
- Request a recommendation from a trusted professional.

- Using a word processing program, write the text for your 500-character Specialties section. Spell-check it and post it to your profile.
- Import your contacts and connect with colleagues and classmates.
- Post a status update that is helpful and/or shows expertise.

Week 6

- Accept any invitations that meet your acceptance criteria.
- Write a recommendation for someone in your network.
- Join five more groups.
- Find a helpful PDF, Word, or Excel document and post it to Box.net files.
- Find a helpful PowerPoint and post it to SlideShare or Google Presentation.
- Document your key network statistics and make a note to periodically record and compare those numbers to track your progress.
- Download the Outlook Toolbar.
- Ask for an introduction from one of your connections using the LinkedIn Introduction feature.
- Post a status update that is helpful and/or shows expertise.
- Document your specific LinkedIn goals for the next quarter.

Once you have completed this six-week game plan, your compelling profile (including enthusiastic recommendations) and significant number of connections will allow you to consistently be found by people who are searching on LinkedIn. Your use of the search function will enable you to continually find new connections and locate valuable information. And joining groups and getting involved in group discussions will help you continue to expand your presence on LinkedIn.

As you make updates to your profile and more thoroughly develop your LinkedIn strategy, remember that effective networking begins with sharing your knowledge and resources with others. So you should periodically add helpful documents on your profile, and use frequent status updates to share interesting articles, websites, and other information with your network. In the networking world, nice guys finish first!

Managing Your Time on LinkedIn

Just like clockwork, toward the end of each of my LinkedIn classes, someone brings up the issue of time management. The questions typically include:

- How much time should I spend on LinkedIn?
- What should I do with that time?
- How do I make my time on LinkedIn productive?
- How can I be sure I am being productive and achieving my goals?

I have found that the most effective way to manage the amount of time spent on LinkedIn is to follow daily, weekly, and monthly to-do lists. You can expect all of these tasks to take a total of about two to three hours each week, but spending even more time can result in greater value. Trust me—your time investment in LinkedIn will pay dividends. The following to-do lists will help you reach the highest level of effectiveness while keeping the time you spend on LinkedIn at a manageable level.

Daily LinkedIn To Do's

- Review your home page.
- Respond to any messages in your inbox.
- Respond to any invitations to join other people's networks.
- Review your Network Activity section to check for interesting events, projects, or comments.
- Check discussions in your two or three most important industry groups.
- Invite people you met the previous day to join your network, as long as they are people you know and trust or you are going to make sure you get together with them to discuss each other's goals and objectives.
- Post a link to a helpful article, blog post, or website in your status box.

Weekly LinkedIn To Do's

- Look at Events to see if anyone has posted an event you should attend.
- Search for events in your region that you might be interested in attending.
- Look at updates your connections have made to their Recommendations section.
- Look at new groups that your connections are joining.
- Review profile updates of the most important people in your network.
- Review the new connections of your Number 1 connections.
- Look at the complete networks of any new Number 1's.
- Review the results of your three saved searches.
- Post any relevant articles, blog posts, or events on your most important groups.

Monthly LinkedIn To Do's

- Review your profile for possible additions or changes.
- Review your list of first-level connections and identify people you should contact in the near future.
- Consider revising any of your three saved searches for increased effectiveness.
- Go through your connections list and write two unsolicited recommendations.
- Make a list of people who may derive real benefit from being connected to each other and set up a lunch or breakfast to introduce them.

Periodic To Do's (Every Few Months)

- Review individual and company profiles of your closest competitors.
- Save and print the latest copy of your profile.
- Save and print your connections list.

You will want to save and print your profile and list of connections as a safety precaution; I have heard a few stories about data being lost on the LinkedIn site. This is not a common occurrence, but taking the time to safeguard this information is well worth the effort.

Regularly maintaining and monitoring your LinkedIn presence will be instrumental in helping you to meet and exceed your professional goals—whether that be advancing your personal brand, selling your goods and services, or finding a job. And remember—all this can be done while lounging on your living room sofa and keeping an eye on your favorite TV program. Who says it's only the young people who can multitask!

CHAPTER 20

Conclusion (Or Is It Just the Beginning?)

Which Camp Are You In?

You did it. You got to the final chapter of what is probably your first book about the new world of social media. I am honored that you spent those hours listening to me, a 53-year-old furniture guy, share business experiences I've had over the years. I hope you will apply them to this state-of-the-art tool and improve and expand your marketing and branding efforts.

Now that you've finished the book, you may be wondering, *How could this guy have over 1,100 people he considers trusted professionals?* That's a completely legitimate question. I do a significant amount of teaching as part of my LinkedIn business, and many of those who attend my seminars are job seekers. It is my nature to be an encourager. I like to help people. Therefore, I occasionally allow people to join my network even though I probably met them quickly after one of my presentations. Later, when

I find out they are connected to someone who is putting up a million-cubicle building, I am hopeful that they will introduce me to their friend because of the value they received from my training. I have yet to receive that dream order, but many of these casual introductions have subsequently developed into valuable and trusted relationships.

When I teach my LinkedIn training class for beginners, my goal is to get rid of the fear factor, and as I mentioned in the introductory chapter, that was my goal with this book as well. I truly hope I have allayed any fear you may have had about LinkedIn. I also stated in the introduction that upon finishing this book, you would end up in one of three camps. Let's revisit those three options before you get on with your marketing and branding efforts:

Camp Number 1: "Nah, nothin' here. I understand the tool and its capabilities. It might be good for others, but it's not really for me." At least you now know what your competitors may be doing. Tell your friends and associates who want to connect with you on LinkedIn that you have decided to do your marketing and branding in other ways that you feel more closely fit your skill set and your schedule.

Camp Number 2: "I am going to put LinkedIn on the back burner and possibly use one or two features." If you are in the second camp, you can continue your investigation into LinkedIn by doing one or more of the following:

- Ask some of your trusted friends and associates who spend time on LinkedIn, "What are you specifically doing on LinkedIn and what results have you seen as a result of your efforts?"
- Attend a workshop presented by an experienced LinkedIn trainer.

- Be on the lookout for specific examples and evidence of ways LinkedIn may help you achieve some of your marketing and branding goals.
- Consider bringing in a marketing intern for the summer or for a semester to do a thorough investigation into your competition's LinkedIn presence and activity.
- If you are involved in industry associations or peer groups, suggest that the topic of LinkedIn be presented and debated for the good of all members. You will not be alone in wanting to talk about LinkedIn—I promise!

Camp Number 3: "I get it, I can do this, and I want to do this!" The majority of the people I encounter land in this camp. If you fall here too, you see significant benefits of planning and executing a LinkedIn strategy—and possibly strategies for other social media tools as well. However, you may still be hesitant to make the commitment because you have a busy life and are not sure you want to have to stay on top of another inbox when you could be pursuing your favorite leisure activity. This is where the rubber meets the road. This is where attitude and commitment have to kick in. If you are going to embrace LinkedIn and the changes it will bring to how you do business, you need to believe that you will receive real value as a result of the time and effort you devote to developing a presence on LinkedIn.

From my firsthand experience and the reports I have received from people who have embraced LinkedIn, measurable results are typically obtained within two to three months of signing up. Your commitment will pay off, but, as with any kind of networking, patience and diligence are required. Just keep in mind that LinkedIn allows you to grow your network exponentially, and every new connection you make puts you closer to closing that million-cubicle deal.

As your network grows, it is important to continue developing your professional relationships, and sharing your knowledge about the extraordinary capabilities of LinkedIn is one way to do so. Share your success stories with friends and business associates, and show them how to use the LinkedIn features you have found to be most useful.

Throughout this book I have discussed the Power Formula and what it means to you as a business professional. Remember, your **unique experience** plus your **unique relationships** plus this **tool** (LinkedIn) equals the **power** to execute your business plan at the highest level. LinkedIn may be the newest and shiniest tool in your toolbox, but it can only be effective if you combine it with **what** you already know and **who** you already know. So start connecting today!

My Kids Are Already on Facebook—Can't They Find a Job There?

Why College Students Need to Be on LinkedIn

As the father of three extraordinary daughters, I have experienced the full range of parental emotions—from the highs of birth, first steps, and scoring that first soccer goal, to the lows of the first car accident and less-than-stellar boyfriend. But the top-of-the-mountain moment was the phone call I received from my oldest daughter: "I got a full-time job, Dad, with benefits!"

If you are the parent of an unemployed or soon-to-be college graduate or have a friend who would like to get a kid on his or her way to financial independence, this chapter is for you.

LinkedIn can be quite beneficial when searching for an internship or permanent position, and it can help young people build a solid "professional personal brand." This is the term I use to describe a person's brand in the business marketplace; it is about the person him- or herself and should not be confused with a company's brand or with personal brands on sites like Facebook, which may not be very professional.

Not so many years ago, the phrase "personal branding" was not even part of our professional language, but these days most people realize they need a personal brand in order to succeed. What changed? First, people are not staying in jobs as long as they did when my father and grandfather were in the workforce. In those days, you stayed with a company for a long, long time, and your personal brand was directly tied to the company for which you worked. It had little to do with you as an individual. Nowadays, the average worker holds many more positions throughout his or her adult life, and one job does not define a career.

Second, technology has allowed people to have a very extensive virtual presence, which can impact what they are trying to accomplish in the business world both positively and negatively. Young people are joining social networking sites at the ages of ten, eleven, and twelve years old, but many of these kids fail to recognize how their actions, discussions, and other information they post can negatively affect their future personal and professional brands. On the other hand, these social networking tools, if used responsibly, can play a very positive role in developing a strong personal brand.

Here are the top ten reasons young people should be on LinkedIn prior to graduating from college:

1. They are already on Facebook and other social networking sites, so they will grasp LinkedIn more quickly than people in my age group. Because the sites operate so similarly, it will not be hard for college students to trade some of their

Facebook time for LinkedIn time in order to advance their professional presence in social media.

2. LinkedIn is perhaps the only social networking site a young person's future employer is actually active on. If business executives choose only one social networking site, they typically choose LinkedIn—so young job seekers definitely want to make sure they have a profile there. To assist potential employers in finding him, remind the young person to include his LinkedIn URL on his resume, cover letters, and e-mail signature.

3. LinkedIn allows users to review and print the profile of the person with whom they are going to interview prior to calling or meeting her. This is an invaluable resource in helping interviewees understand who the person is and finding areas of potential discussion and commonality for their upcoming interview. Remind the young person that the businessperson who wrote that profile is proud of every bit of information included in it. Understanding and remembering it will result in a much richer conversation during the interview, which should give him a competitive advantage over the other candidates for the job.

4. Encourage the young person to prepare a video resume and have her place the link to it in the Websites section, the SlideShare application, or the Google Presentation application. Video resumes are a powerful differentiator for college students, because not only can they go into more detail about their specific accomplishments, but they can also show their personality and passion for their current projects and future goals.

5. LinkedIn allows students to make connections in college that will give their upcoming job search a huge boost. They may say, *Yeah, but I don't know anybody in business, so how can I really go about putting together that muskie net you talked about?* Recommend that they connect with their fellow students, and remind them that the idea is not just to add more Level 1 connections but also the 2's and 3's to which those Level 1's are connected. The minute a student connects with her roommate, she could be adding all the business executives her roommate's parents know into her network. College students should also be connecting with friends of their parents or family members who are tied into the business community. That will allow them to begin having conversations with more seasoned professionals about what the student hopes to accomplish as he or she approaches graduation. Adding fellow students and family friends in the business community is one way to begin a successful business networking career.

6. Students can use LinkedIn to search for internships. Chances are the company he or she wants to get an upcoming summer internship with is on LinkedIn. The student may be fortunate enough to find the specific person he wants to meet, but, if not, he may at least find people in the same department. He can then figure out if someone he knows is connected to those people. Most internships are found through networking, not through answering ads, and LinkedIn can give young people a head start on the networking they need to do in order to find that perfect internship. Students can also use the LinkedIn Jobs function to search for internships.

7. When a student begins her formal job search in earnest, LinkedIn will allow her to look for the people she wants to sit down with to discuss the kind of job she is looking for and how she might go about getting it. These people will function as career mentors to her, and she will have a lot more opportunities to find the right mentors if she is connected to the right people on LinkedIn.

8. LinkedIn can help students find recruiters who are involved in the industry in which they hope to find their first job. Recruiters love LinkedIn and are very active on it. Having an excellent profile also increases the chances of recruiters finding the student.

9. LinkedIn can be used as the student's home page or personal website. It can bring together all of the social networking sites he uses (his blog and his accounts with Twitter, Flickr, Facebook, etc.). However, he will want to be certain that the information posted on these other sites is in line with the professional image he wants to portray. His future employer does not want to hear about his experience hosting parties with beer bongs and bikinis; that type of information can ruin his chances at a job.

10. LinkedIn allows students to list all of their volunteer work, college leadership experiences, and committees on which they served. This will help to differentiate them from students who have been less active while attending college. When the student is looking for a job immediately following her graduation from college, she probably won't have a lot of formal job experience; these leadership positions and volunteer opportunities set her apart in the eyes of

potential employers. Remember, she gets 2,000 characters for each job and educational entry on her profile. Figure BC.1 shows the volunteer work I've included in my profile. If the student has had these types of experiences, remind her to take full advantage of the Experience section as a way to exhibit her worth to potential employers or individuals who could assist her in her job search.

As valuable as LinkedIn and other social media tools can be in achieving personal and professional goals, they can be equally detrimental if a person's online presence is inconsistent with his or her actual personality and character. College is the best time to begin thinking about who you are, what you stand for, and what type of company you wish to affiliate yourself with, and LinkedIn can get students started towards that positive, powerful, "professional personal brand" that will stick with them throughout their career.

Figure BC.1: Employers value a young person's service to the community.

Current	• Office Furniture Dealership President & Owner (Preferred Haworth Office Furniture Dealer) at M&M Office Interiors [Edit] • Founder & Linkedin Trainer at Power Formula [Edit] • Board Member & Volunteer Instructor at Make A Difference-Wisconsin [Edit] • Board Member at The Community Warehouse [Edit] • Volunteer High School Mentor at Urban Promise Lunch Club [Edit] see less... ✚ Add Current Position
Past	• Volunteer Youth Leader at Eastbrook Church • Executive Vice President at Russ Darrow Automotive Group • Vice President at Heiser Automotive Group • Manager Small Business Division at Arthur Andersen & Co see less...

APPLYING THE POWER FORMULA

- Even though the young person in your life may be just begin-ning his professional career, he already has **unique expe-riences** that could be very helpful to him in his upcoming job search. Internships, organizational involvement (espe-cially leadership positions), and summer employment can be explained on his LinkedIn profile in such a way that they will show prospective employers that the student is the type of strong candidate they are looking for.

- Employers aren't the only ones who can write recommenda-tions. Leaders of organizations, teachers, and professors can also help students substantiate some of the **unique experi-ences** they have had through a testimonial on LinkedIn.

- LinkedIn applications and some of the other profile features discussed in this book can help students more effectively con-vey their collegiate experience in ways that will differentiate them from other candidates. Understanding and using these tools could significantly enhance the student's ability to tell the story of his or her **unique experience**. Plus, proficiency on LinkedIn is a skill that many employers will regard as leading edge.

- Students' **unique relationships** with teachers, parents, men-tors, and other students can lead to second- or third-degree connections that may help them land that important interview.

Acknowledgments

What a wild ride it has been—writing a social media book at age fifty-three. I couldn't have done it without the help of the following people:

Brenda (my wife, best friend, grammar czar)—You have been the inspiration for the book in so many ways—from your beginning declaration, "We should write a book," to your many, many hours of typing, proofing, editing, convincing, and, most importantly, persevering. You're great!

Erica, Jenna, and Deanna (my daughters and personal consultants for "all things computer," graphic design, and Facebook generation philosophy)—Simply put, you guys rock!

Wayne and Marge Breitbarth (my parents)—Even though you will never be on LinkedIn and perhaps never read more than this page of my book, your living examples of what it means to be a friend, business owner, and parent have had an immeasurable influence on the experiences and perspectives that I share throughout the book. I love you!

Tim Rudd (my partner and good friend)—Thanks for being the most understanding partner a guy could have during my exploration of LinkedIn.

Bob Hetzel (my faithful friend)—Your constant encouragement, whether hiking in Colorado or making business and life decisions, always motivates me to get to the top.

Todd Schwerm (my good friend and first LinkedIn connection)—Without your persistence in telling me "You've gotta join LinkedIn," I would not be writing this book. Thanks for caring so much about me.

Joe Guidi (Mini Me)—Your youthful insights about how younger business professionals think and act have helped me every step of the way. You are wise beyond your years.

Jack Covert (business book author and founder of 800-CEO-READ)—Without your taking my phone call ("Wayne who?"), spending time talking about my book, and ultimately recommending Greenleaf Book Group, the final product would not be what it is. Thanks also for helping businesspeople across the country know what business books to spend our precious time on.

The Team at Greenleaf Book Group (my publisher)—Thanks to all of you for sharing your expertise and skills and for having the patience to answer my many questions. Clint, you have put together a team of real professionals who care.

Jason Alba—Your book *I'm on LinkedIn—Now What???* started me down this path. I don't know whether to curse you or hug you, so I will stick with the latter. Thanks for being a pioneer.

Jan Vermeiren—Your book *How to REALLY Use LinkedIn* helped me get to the aha moment of realizing you'd better have a strategy on all this social media stuff or not waste your time.

Neal Schaffer—Your book *Windmill Networking: Understanding, Leveraging & Maximizing LinkedIn* and your blog posts are my continuing source of "go deep" information on everything LinkedIn.

Gary Vaynerchuk—As I am writing this with my "Crush It" wristband on, I am thankful for the inspiration your book and videos have given me to do just that—crush it.

Erik Qualman—Your book *Socialnomics* was the first book I read that connected the dots for me on how social media works from a 35,000-foot view. Thanks also for your video "Social Media Revolution," which is a powerful closer for many of my social media presentations.

David Meerman Scott—Had I not devoured *The New Rules of Marketing and PR*, I would not have come to the realization that we are all thought leaders at something, and the Internet is our way to be able to create a "worldwide rave."

My Early Audiences (my guinea pigs)—I can't believe you had any interest in listening to a CPA/office furniture guy talk to you about something you wanted nothing to do with and then told your friends to do the same. I couldn't have and wouldn't have wanted to do this without your encouragement.

Pepsi Max (my caffeine elixir)—I don't know that I could have gotten through all the writing and editing without the extra caffeine and ginseng with which you are so lovingly loaded.

Jesus (my Lord and Savior)—Your example of how to connect with people is the standard for which we should all strive.

Index

FOR MORE INFORMATION . . .

VISIT www.powerformula.net to:

- Receive notices of updates to this book
- Download free resources
- Subscribe to Wayne's Weekly Tips & Helps
- View video clips
- Link to other resources (including training DVDs)
- See what others are saying about *The Power Formula for LinkedIn Success*

FOLLOW Wayne on Twitter at twitter.com/WayneBreitbarth for daily LinkedIn tips.

JOIN the conversation by becoming a member of the Power Formula LinkedIn group.

CONTACT Wayne at wayne@powerformula.net to learn more about the valuable services he provides, including:

- Corporate consulting and training
- Keynote presentations for conventions, conferences, and corporate events. See Wayne's energetic and humorous presentation style at www.youtube.com/user/wbreitbarth.

About the Author

Wayne Breitbarth is an owner of M&M Office Interiors in Pewaukee, Wisconsin. Prior to his involvement in the office furniture business, he spent nearly twenty years in the automotive industry. He received his BBA from the University of Wisconsin-Whitewater and his MBA from Marquette University. Wayne is also a Certified Public Accountant and spent the early years of his career as an auditor and small business consultant with Arthur Andersen & Co.

Throughout his career, Wayne has been involved with a number of philanthropic organizations. His financial background has enabled him to assist Make A Difference-Wisconsin in its mission to enrich the community by empowering high school students to make sound financial decisions. His work with this organization includes serving on its board of directors as well as teaching financial literacy classes to students in Milwaukee Public Schools. He is also the founder of Urban Promise, an urban youth mentoring program that brings together business professionals and high school students in Milwaukee

Public Schools. Wayne also serves on the board of directors of the Community Warehouse, a nonprofit organization that serves the Milwaukee community by providing affordable home- and facility-improvement materials. He is a member of the Milwaukee Area Technical College's Accounting Careers advisory board and has served as a youth leader and teacher at Eastbrook Church in Milwaukee.

Wayne's work with urban youth has been applauded by the Wisconsin Institute of Certified Public Accountants, and he proudly accepted the 2009 WICPA Public Service Award.

Wayne began moonlighting as a LinkedIn trainer in early 2009 and has now led seminars for nearly 10,000 business professionals. He has inspired audiences both locally, at many of Milwaukee's most prominent companies and organizations, and nationally, at conventions, industry association events, and corporate training sessions. Wayne's diverse business experience, pragmatic teaching style, and infectious sense of humor have earned him the praise of the press and the distinction of being referred to as the "LinkedIn Guru."

Wayne resides in Milwaukee, Wisconsin, with his wife of thirty years. They have three daughters.